CRITICAL THINKING FOR ADDICTION PROFESSIONALS

About the Author

MICHAEL J. TALEFF, PHD, CSAC, MAC, is an instructor at the University of Hawai'i at Manoa and West O'ahu, and National University (Hawaii Branch). He was the first editor of the *Journal of Teaching in Addictions,* and served two terms as president of the International Coalition for Addiction Studies Education (INCASE). Dr. Taleff is also the author of numerous articles and chapters, as well as *A Handbook to Access and Treat Resistance in Chemical Dependency,* and co-author of *A Recovery Workbook: The Road Back from Substance Abuse.* He conducts critical thinking research within the addiction field, and presents widely on the topic of critical thinking in addiction treatment.

Critical Thinking for Addiction Professionals

MICHAEL J. TALEFF, PhD, CSAC, MAC

Springer Publishing Company, Inc.
11 West 42nd Street
New York, NY 10036

Acquisitions Editor: Lauren Dockett
Production Editor: Jeanne Libby
Cover design by Mimi Flow
Typeset by Daily Information Processing, Churchville, PA

06 07 08 09 10 / 5 4 3 2 1

Library of Congress Cataloging-in-Publication Data

Taleff, Michael J.
Critical thinking for addiction professionals / Michael J. Taleff.
p. ; cm.
Includes bibliographical references and index.
ISBN 0-8261-1824-0
1. Clinical psychology—Decision making. 2. Counseling—Decision making. 3. Decision making.
[DNLM: 1. Counseling—methods. 2. Behavior, Addictive. 3. Judgment. 4. Perception. 5. Substance-Related Disorders—therapy. WM 55 T143c 2006] I. Title.

RC457.T35 2006
616.89—dc22

2005029679

Printed in the United States of America by Bang Printing.

To Audrey Elaine Taleff,
an extraordinarily loving, bright, dedicated human

Contents

Preface

Bill, a well-meaning and experienced addiction counselor for fifteen years, has just walked out of a typical addiction counseling session. He believes he did a good job but actually, he made a number of mistakes, and he doesn't even know it. The mistakes he made were linked to critical thinking errors he often commits. Those errors, in turn, led him to recommend a set of bad clinical decisions for his client.

Now, Bill is a fairly bright guy. He is certified in his state, and has received good evaluations from his supervisor. He trusts that he thinks well, but sometimes, he doesn't. For example, in the case he just left, Bill assessed his client as having a significant alcohol problem, based on only one symptom. Bill then jumped to a clinical decision that sent the client to an intensive inpatient program. The more appropriate approach would have been to conduct further evaluations, contact individuals (family members, employer, etc.) to gather additional information, and then make a clinical decision as to treatment.

Decisions like this happen all the time because flawed thinking leads to erroneous conclusions. This is only one part of the critical thinking problem in the addiction field. The same thinking errors happen at the supervisory and administrative levels. That is, supervisors and administrators make the same kinds of generalizing mistakes by jumping to conclusions before investigating reasonable options.

Another area of the addiction field has similar problems. For example, I have attended numerous workshops and conferences and have read many addiction books over the years. Walking out of some conferences or finishing some books left me believing, "That was pretty good. It made sense." Walking out of other conferences and finishing other books left me thinking, "That wasn't quite right. Those explanations were not well connected."

The more I pondered these reactions the clearer it became to me that statements made by counselors, supervisors, administrators, authors, and presenters were often the result of more than a few thinking flaws.

I asked others how they felt after they talked with colleagues or attended workshops and read books on addiction. Lo and behold, many agreed with my impressions. They also thought certain things did not ring true. Those problems turned out to be associated with thinking flaws.

I also observed many kinds of thinking flaws in the numerous staff meetings I attended over the years. I saw bad clinical decisions being made by so-called trained, experienced, and certified counselors. These poor decisions led to equally poor strategies that were passed on to clients.

Some people in the field believe they have arrived at a fundamental truth about addiction science, but many of them have bought into a pernicious set of fallacies. Those fallacies have then been transmitted to others and have clung to them like a bad hangover, constantly distorting their thinking. Such "truths" have been known to mesmerize people for decades.

How do we go about protecting ourselves from this barrage of fallacies? That question gave rise to this book. The result is a collection of ideas that can shield all of us from bad thinking. The goal is to think well so that better clinical outcomes will follow.

There is a temptation to grab power in professing one's ideas and beliefs. I have made a strong attempt to limit my personal bias in this book and I cannot recommend strongly enough that readers make up their own minds about issues in our field and in this book. Should you wish to debate a point I have made by all means contact me and let the debate begin.

I've also made it a point to illustrate concepts with examples from my own experiences as well as those of colleagues. You will notice that the chapters are written in a clinical style not usually found in critical thinking books. But this book is intended for clinicians and other addiction professionals, so it incorporates explanations about motivation and behavior that foster critical and non-critical thinking in clinical settings.

Thought is human nature (Youngson, 1998). To be vigilant against behaviors and motivations that interfere with clear thought is a step out of darkness. This book offers no particular answers, only ideas that can lead to higher levels of clarification in thinking (Warburton, 2004). Using these ideas, readers can better assess the quality of their work and perhaps gauge the development of their own thought.

Although critical thinking has been applied to allied fields such as nursing, social work, and psychology, I believe this is a first-of-its-kind book for the general addiction field. It is long overdue.

The book is divided into two main sections. Part one, the first six chapters, serve as a broad introduction to critical thinking: what it is, how it can serve the addiction field, and things that get in the way of good thinking. Part II, the last six chapters, discuss the various thinking fallacies that interfere with addiction decision making. Each of these chapters has examples that cast more light on the way these fallacies create problems for the addiction field. Part II ends with a short chapter on the ethics and consequences for using critical thinking, and advice about the consequences of implementing critical thinking.

Acknowledgments

I wish to acknowledge Marguerite Babcock. Our early discussions set the stage for this endeavor. I would also like to acknowledge Lauren Dockett at Springer Publishing for her faith in this project.

PART I

Introduction and Basics

CHAPTER ONE

Introducing Critical Thinking Into Addiction Work

You are invited to experience a form of thinking that can enhance your professional skills, expertise, and development. It has the potential to improve all areas of your counseling: from the assessment phase, to the selection of counseling strategies, to discharge. It can make you a better supervisor and administrator. It also has the capacity to propel you to consider new ideas and use methods of investigation you may have only imagined. Critical thinking will help you make better sense of our world, and especially the people you hope to help.

PUTTING THINGS IN CONTEXT

As humans, we all start out uncertain and amazed with everything around us. We learn to understand the world and its people by following the beliefs of religion, philosophy, and science (Charpak & Broch, 2004). From those fields we create our own theories of why things happen and why people do what they do. We are fascinated by the nature of humans and are constantly trying to figure out what makes people tick. Some experts believe this practice is imbedded in our psyches (Pinker, 2002). Consider how much "figuring out" or thinking goes into counseling. For example, addiction professionals observe clients and try to make sense of why they do the things they do. We assess a vast amount of information. Then we attempt to form a workable hypothesis that will best describe the dynamics of a case. We judge our treatment strategies as to effectiveness. And every working day, we sort out a host of other developments that need deliberation. Such thought requires as few mental contaminants as possible. As you use critical thinking principles, you will begin to recognize the myriad of fallacious thinking processes that bombard you every day. They come from a variety of sources, including television, the printed page, and certainly the Internet. Clear thinking will allow you to make better clinical decisions, and better personal ones as well. With practice, your mind will become sharper.

These central themes direct the main points of this book:

- Understanding the importance of critical thinking
- Explaining the connection between critical thinking and passion
- Showing that critical thinking, sometimes assumed to be a boring subject, is quite stimulating
- Spelling out why critical thinking is vital to all aspects of the addiction field
- Presenting a few easy-to-understand critical thinking definitions
- Reviewing a few critical thinking procedures
- Reviewing a list of fallacies that interfere with clinical thinking
- Presenting a few warnings concerning the price to pay for being a critical thinker.

WHAT IS THE POINT OF UNDERSTANDING CRITICAL THINKING?

Questions comprise much of practice in critical thinking and a good way to start a book on the subject is to ask a basic one: Why would anyone spend time trying to understand critical thinking? A major reason is discovery. It can mean discovering things about our clients so we can better assess and engage them. It can also teach us how to run a program effectively. Trying to discover why you think the way you do, or self-discovery, leads to personal growth, and that is always a welcome goal. Yet, this road to discovery is not about filling your brain with the latest pop psychology fads. Those methods simply call for you to acquire information and to do it without much inquiry. This "fill your mind" approach is promoted in many self-help books, addiction-oriented lectures, and workshops. This book asks you to go beyond acquiring mere information. It asks you to deliberate on what you hear and read.

Another major reason to engage in critical thinking comes from the philosopher Immanuel Kant. Two hundred years ago, he noted that the human mind never quite seems to get a clear picture of the world. According to Kant, the mind always registers the world indirectly because any perception or thought is filtered through our preconceived notions or mental sets (Magee, 1998; Mole, 2002; Warburton, 2004). For our purposes, this means that we need to be acutely aware that these notions contain our own little bits of bias, which distort the way we perceive the world.

Knowing that bias exists, we need to ask the important clinical question: What in my mind is filtering the facts about my clients? Many theories offered to the addiction field may only be someone's ideas about addiction; those ideas had to be filtered through a set of that person's own preconceived notions. In any case, the result is not a clear picture of people or addiction. To get a clear picture you need to know the reasons for what you believe and the implications of such beliefs (Fisher, 2001).

Addiction counselors and supervisors with weak critical thinking skills may be susceptible to using unsubstantiated or thoughtless clinical procedures that will harm the client. The good news is that these limitations can be corrected to some extent by critical thinking.

It bears repeating that a vital reason to use critical thinking is to see your clients as clearly as possible, and then base your clinical decisions on that clear thinking (Gambrill, 1990). To do anything less borders on the unethical.

You may be thinking that you already know how to think. To some degree this is true. However, unless you checked it out lately, your thinking may not be all that effective (Stanovich, 2002). All thinking can use a little tune-up.

One last point needs to be made. Improving thinking does not require that you be a genius. A normal level of intelligence will do just fine (Allen, 1998). If you understood this paragraph, you can understand anything in this book.

MORE REASONS TO UNDERSTAND CRITICAL THINKING

Through the years I have observed that addiction professionals have a tendency to judge something they read or hear really fast and at a gut level. They come to a conclusion without pause for thought, good reasons, or evidence. Moreover, these same people are proud to make these speedy, intuitive types of judgments. "I have a gut feeling about that" is an often-heard catchphrase. Many counselors who act on these gut feelings actually believe they think clearly. Making quick judgments without pausing to reflect, or jumping to conclusions without a good set of reasons is not clear thinking. Mindless judgments do not bring about true discoveries (Langer, 1989).

In this book, you are asked to withhold those un-thoughtful and rapid gut impressions. Instead, you are encouraged to really think about what you read and the people you observe. This reflective thinking is the way to find the true values and assumptions behind what you read and see (Kurland, 1995). You are advised not to accept ideas based on speculation or intuition without some good reasons to believe (Magee, 1998). (That also goes for the ideas expressed in this book.)

With that comes a challenge to you: to understand and interpret as clearly as possible the meanings behind your thinking and the thinking of others. Although some may try, nobody can frivolously opt out of critical thinking by simply self-righteously justifying his or her own reasoning processes (Craig, 2002; Stevenson & Haberman, 1998). Some people may even go so far as to claim that thinking isn't important to their clinical work, or that their clinical conclusions don't warrant an explanation. This attitude is no longer adequate for today's addiction field.

Well thought out ideas are the real discoveries to be made in this world, and the tools to get to many of those discoveries come from critical thinking. For instance, suppose you finish this book and find out that you can make better judgments, better clinical assessments, and better evaluations about people in general and clients in particular. What if you find out that your thinking has become crisp, more insightful? Because of these thinking improvements you can then start to make better personal decisions and start to feel better about yourself. Imagine the things you could do with that kind of clarity and internal confidence—the journeys you could take and the innovative things you could do!

This is the enticement to you. Drop a few preconceptions, add a different twist to your usual thinking, and watch what truly interesting things will begin to take place.

THE PASSION WITHIN A CRITICAL MIND

Before we continue, it is important to say a few words about an unjust prejudice aimed at critical thinking. It is the notion that critical thinkers are somehow distant, cool, and aloof. This prejudice also assumes that becoming a critical thinker will somehow make you an emotional prune and that possessing a critical temperament is un-therapeutic.

What a set of myths!

Critical thinkers can be as passionate and emotional as anyone else (Cannovo, 1998). Brookfield (1987) notes that critical thinkers can feel joy, relief, and the exhilaration that comes from perceiving new ways of looking at the world.

Becoming a critical thinker in no way demands that you drop your emotions. No person, living or dead, has ever achieved that, and it is practically impossible to think without some level of emotion (Hughes, 2000). Rather, critical thinking encourages you to avoid being led by emotions. Critical thinkers learn to corral and draw on their emotional power to increase their productivity, better themselves, and those around them, plus enhance their chosen field.

Rather than considering thinking as some kind of unemotional process, view the rationally trained mind as something that will increase your passion. To deeply think about something requires you to invest time, thought, and emotion in the process. Solomon (1999) claims that people are never more themselves than when they think and care intensely about something. Passion that comes from critical thinking is not about denying emotions or repressing them; it is about cultivating and regulating them (Solomon, 1999).

ISN'T THIS STUFF DULL?

When you first heard the words "critical thinking," you probably thought the concept ranked up there with some of the most boring things you have ever encountered. To be perfectly blunt, part of that statement is true. Aspects of critical thinking can be dreary. However, once you get the drift of it, this material can open exciting new windows in your mind, letting in fresh air to clear out old cobwebs.

But let's not drop this argument against boredom quite yet. There is one more relevant boredom myth: the way the information is delivered. You know the boring lecture routine. We have all run across those people and books that can make even skydiving boring. This book tries to avoid that style of presentation. It is not technical. It attempts to stay on course and not aimlessly wander. Most important, it is not out to impress. People who try to impress rapidly become bores. The book's prime focus is critical thinking and what it can do.

In my travels, I have seen the excitement on people's faces when they are exposed to critical thinking. This is especially true in addiction professional audiences. Once you figure out a few simple concepts, you just might find your brain coming alive with new ideas that will fire your imagination and stir your soul.

CRITICAL THINKING: A FIRST LOOK

So far we have been building an argument for the importance of critical thinking in terms of personal growth and development in general, and addiction counseling in particular. But, what exactly is critical thinking? We can regard critical thinking as a set of tools for making some interesting and clear discoveries. These tools are methods to explore new ideas, and do it with a purpose (Taleff, 2000). Critical thinking doesn't skew your thought processes to favor a particular outcome (Kurfiss, 1988). The point is rather to improve your thinking and make it clearer, more accurate, and more defensible. Simply, it is thinking about thinking (Paul, 1993).

Now, beware of falling into the trap of believing that the critical thinker is always looking for faults or always looking for a fight (Harnadek, 1998). That is simply not true. True critical thinkers more commonly:

- Try hard to keep an open mind, but not so open that their brains fall out
- Question even their prized beliefs
- Subject such beliefs to a thorough analysis; if the beliefs survive the analysis they are reliable and valid
- Know how to distinguish between good and poor thinking
- Balance emotions and intellect
- Do not argue something if they know little about the subject
- Gather information to fill in any knowledge gaps
- Know that people from different cultures, regions, and age ranges have different ideas and different meanings for words, and take these factors into account when they critically analyze
- Have little tolerance for passing off poorly constructed ideas to others
- Admit when they are wrong
- Applaud well-formed thought
- Attempt, in small and large ways, to make a difference in the world.

HOW CAN CRITICAL THINKING BENEFIT ADDICTION COUNSELING?

There are a number of explanations of how critical thinking can benefit addiction counseling. High on this list is the fact that good clinical decisions require solid reasoning skills. If I am making one poor clinical decision after another, how can I expect the overall direction of counseling to be positive? It is worth repeating that bad thinking produces bad clinical judgments (Gambrill, 1990; Taleff, 2000). Poor judgments, in turn, affect the quality of counseling (Carlson, 1995). Research indicates that positive counseling outcomes correlate well with better critical reasoning (Gambrill, 1990).

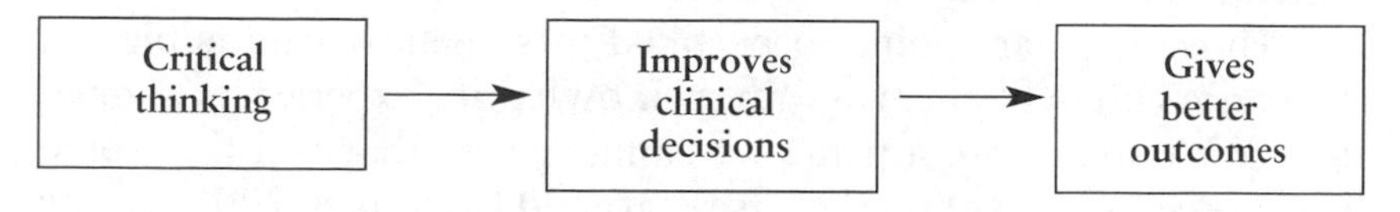

One more benefit of using critical thinking in counseling is that it fosters the ability to be constructive and creative (Tavris & Wade, 1995). The constructive element is demonstrated by how the addiction professional comes up with more valid explanations for clients and program administration than those supplied by non-critical thinkers. The creative element is revealed through more innovative options to fit the needs of the client and facility.

A FIRST LOOK AT WHAT DRIVES POOR THINKING

We need to pause and ask what propels poor clinical thinking in the first place? There are reasons we don't think well. In fact, there are quite a number of reasons for poor thinking. Many are addressed later in this book. But, for now, let's just step back and look at how the simple process of getting to know our clients might contribute to poor thinking.

This process often starts with not knowing that one has a head full of uncritical thinking patterns. Under such conditions, there is never a thought or need to examine how one arrives at certain conclusions (Mole, 2002). For example, many counselors generate certain suppositions based on the limited amount of evidence at their disposal. No matter how intensive the assessment, our evaluations of clients can only provide us with imperfect information. All assessments have that failing. Pause for a minute and ask if anyone has the ability to completely know another person. The answer is no. One can never figure out with mathematical precision exactly what is going on in the mind of another person (Edelman, 2004).

This means that there are always gaps in the assessment process. Thus, when it comes time to make a clinical judgment or suggest a treatment direction the gaps force counselors to make a best guess or rely on a working hypothesis. Granted, clinical judgment is more than just an assumption, because counselors have some data (prior records, test results, interview data, etc.) on which to base their guess but herein lies the problem.

Those gaps are going to be filled in somehow, and addiction counselors often fill them in with their own prior experiences and beliefs. We humans are a pattern-seeking species that will find some level of meaning to fit our beliefs (Peat, 2003; Shermer, 2001). If our "filling in" process is biased, then our conclusions will be biased. This is an example of poor thinking. Those gaps need to be filled in with as much clear thinking as possible: critical thinking can do that.

No one in the hard or soft sciences is immune from this filling in the gap problem (Mole, 2002). Medical personnel fall prey to assessment gaps all the time. Sometimes they just don't have all the data they need to make a correct diagnosis. That's why many of us are sent to specialists for more information. If doctors feel confident enough, they make a best estimate as to what treatments will work to resolve the problem. So, if the doctor prescribes a medication and then changes the medication or dosage, it may be because the doctor is refining his or her estimate. Don't be alarmed. Most of the time the deduction is a good one. But sometimes it isn't, and then you can read about it as a lawsuit in the newspapers.

We do something similar in the addiction field, but often add a little twist. For instance, we see a client, complete our assessment, and recommend a certain treatment. In theory, if the plan doesn't work we should refine the treatment. In practice however, many counselors blame the client for not following their directions and proclaim that the individual is in a state of denial (Taleff, 1997). Those counselors fill in their gaps with personal experience and beliefs, which in such cases reinforces the notion that people with an addiction problem are, as a group, stubborn, manipulative, and in denial. This is a prime example of a fallacy called *generalizing*.

There is no hard data yet to support what was just stated, but over the years this picture of clients with an addiction has grown to be so iconic that many addiction counselors automatically view all their clients through this lens. To push this point, many addiction counselors are confident that the way they perceive a client is accurate. They believe the form of counseling they use will work for all or almost all cases they encounter. If it doesn't, they often become frustrated. Frustration combines with other negative emotions to block clear thinking. At this point, heightened emotions can result in even more thinking fallacies. In reality, each client is unique and requires unique interventions.

We have a propensity to fill in assessment gaps with our prior ideas and emotions, which distort the reality of the client's situation. However, by using the principles of critical thinking you will be encouraged not to fill in those gaps with distortions. A decrease in distortions will create an atmosphere for better clinical decisions (Stanovich, 2002).

MORE REASONS TO USE CRITICAL THINKING IN THE ADDICTION FIELD

As an addiction professional, I want what's best for my clients. That means trying to supply the most error-free therapy as I possibly can. In other words, I need to make educated responses to complex clients who walk into my office. If counselors make bad decisions (and they will), they can and will put forward inappropriate strategies to clients. This includes using forms of treatment that do more harm than good.

On a larger scale, some professionals spread unfounded beliefs and biases to other addiction counselors, much like a virus. They do it through books, workshops, and even in teaching. Digesting so much unfounded information, good-hearted counselors can be led astray and end up practicing unsubstantiated treatment methods for years, to the detriment of their clients.

These viruses are spreading because many addiction professionals accept a lot of claims about the nature of addiction or the methods to treat it without questioning. (We will say more about this virus problem later.) The lack of questioning leads to more problems (Dauer, 1989). We all have a hard enough time treating addictions without having to follow the errors and deceptions professed by someone else.

This book does not claim that people in the addiction field or counseling in general deliberately practice deception. The point is that honest, caring counselors can be led astray by bad information. For example, many years ago I became the clinical supervisor for an inpatient program. Just prior to my hiring, the head of the program brought in a black box with some protruding wires and claimed that if you hooked clients to this contraption it would reduce cravings in alcoholics. The box was a fake It produced nothing, and he spent a lot of money for nothing. The main problem wasn't the loss of money, but an uncritical appraisal that promised things to clients that were never delivered.

The clients who were attached to this box were told it would do something wonderful for them, and it failed to deliver. Many clients put their faith in bad information, and when it didn't work they returned to abusive drinking. A little critical thinking on the part of the administrator could have avoided this predicament.

That was a fairly blatant example of poor thinking. Yet, other damaging results can occur from poor thinking. For instance:

• Misdiagnosing clients and then applying an unsuitable form of treatment: Misdiagnosis can occur because counselors don't think of other possibilities and jump at the first available solution that comes to mind. For example, a counselor may think a client is subconsciously angry, and the first thing on the counselor's mind is to get the anger "out" by insisting the client punch a pillow or scream at a surrogate parent. Why would counselors resort to this type of treatment? Because a recent workshop told them to do so, and that information was fresh (available) in their minds. (Actually, the data indicate that this form of treatment usually increases the anger [Singer & Lalich, 1996].)

• Not being congruent with a client: Rogers (1957) notes that counselors need to experience themselves deeply and accurately in the counseling session. A head full of bias and fallacious thinking can and will decrease honesty and accuracy.

• Not utilizing a client's strengths and assets: Poor thinking on the part of some addiction counselors makes them conclude that clients with addiction problems don't have strengths because the addiction has bankrupted them of all assets. Yet, clients who survive years of addiction usually have some assets that can be used in the recovery process.

• Sending clients to the wrong treatment setting or to more treatment than is necessary: This comes about because many counselors believe that all people with an addiction, regardless of the extent of the problem, should get the maximum amount of treatment as soon as possible.

• Concentrating on unrelated factors: For example, a counselor can maintain the erroneous belief that all people with an addiction have some repressed memory dynamic at work.

• Thinking the cause of addiction is a simple matter: The counselor will then tell clients that some singular cause resulted in their situation.

In terms of this last item, addiction is quite complex, and there is always more than one possible explanation (Steward & Blocker, 1982). Many factors have to come together to create the problem.

Another example of poor thinking concerns counselor-induced resistance. That's right. Therapists often provoke resistance in counseling. They do this through their own dogmatic beliefs and bad thinking styles. This type of resistance can be reduced when a counselor's judgment is cleaned up via critical thinking (Gambrill, 1990, Taleff, 1997).

Throughout time people have been prone to bad thinking. There are abundant examples of Nobel laureates and other great minds that were easily fooled into believing utterly worthless ideas because they did not think critically. Classic cases include well-educated and high-ranking church officials who almost burned Galileo at the stake for his discovery of moons around Jupiter, and the little-known fact that Isaac Newton (considered by many as the premier scientist of all time) spent a large portion of his life investigating alchemy (Youngson, 1998).

One does not have to search very far to find a profound lack of critical thinking even at college-level addiction coursework, let alone workshops and other forms of training. Faculty can teach a class and assign readings based on biased thinking and they do. Whole departments can adhere to uncritical philosophies. A recent review of curricula across the country indicated that very few offer critical thinking courses (Taleff, 2003).

The last reason for infusing critical thinking into the addiction field is the fact that the field is ready for it. We are progressing at a rapid rate. One only has to look at the books recently published on the subject. Years ago addiction texts relied heavily on personal opinion, authority, and deductive reasoning (making sense of the world from a grand, often flawed, theory to a particular person or thing). These days, addiction books, basing their conclusions on research, have an empirically based approach that attempts to explain how and why addictions occur.

To observe this trend more closely, just note the textbooks being used in many college addiction programs today. In this new scientific light (induction: building a theory on tested facts), more and more addiction professionals are being taught to ask hard, tough questions about what they read and hear. Critical thinking encourages that kind of inquiry. Yet, thinking has always held a suspect place in the addiction field, as we will see in the next section.

AREAS OF STRIFE

Anyone who has worked in the addiction field for a reasonable length of time can tell you a number of stories about contention between some who espouse traditional ideas and methods of treatment and those who would question such ideas and methods and prefer to think things through. Although there has been a certain level of civility and even dialogue between the factions, there have been some downright ugly displays.

To understand this conflict, we first need to see what is bucking heads with what. On one side we have the long-established traditional ideas of treatment and dynamics. On the other side we have principles of critical thinking that question everything, including long-established ideas.

Now, what do we mean by traditional addiction counseling? There are a few key points to the traditional view, which have been outlined by Miller and Rollnick (1991):

- Insisting the client admit and accept that he/she is an addict
- Believing that a disease reduces personal choice and control of addictive substances
- Convincing the client of his/her addiction through perceived evidence that is in the hands of the therapist
- Believing that most, if not all, clients are in some state of denial
- Utilizing confrontation as a main mode of client engagement.

As some of the main points of the traditional perspective, these concepts are often acknowledged as the one and only way to understand and treat addiction with no need for further analysis, judging, or new evidence. The other side would advocate critical thinking as a set of skills used to analyze issues, to look at such issues from all sides, weigh quality evidence, and come to a reasonable judgment that is relatively free from personal bias (Meltzoff, 1998). One can easily see how the traditional and critical thinking perspectives might collide.

A PRIME EXAMPLE OF THE CLASH

Notice in the list above that the fourth item indicates that people with an addiction are in some state of denial. Moreover, according to the traditional view, this defense mechanism never completely disappears, no matter what the client's level of experience in recovery. Denial then, especially in early treatment, is presumed to warp the ability to reason well (Taleff, 1997). Hence the dependent person's thought process is to be viewed with suspicion, and such individuals are often told not to trust themselves because they can fall back into old patterns of "stinkin' thinking."

These thinking patterns utilize other defenses, such as rationalizing or minimizing. Together, these defenses are thought to delude those with a dependency into believing that they can safely drink or drug again. Newly recovering people are also told not to trust their own thinking. Rather, they are encouraged to trust others or program principles. To do otherwise, so goes the logic, is to risk one's sobriety, a warning that has been repeated in countless tales. Although some part of this reasoning process may be true, this advice often generalizes to all thinking, and so is not to be trusted.

At the critical thinking end of this spectrum is the notion that not trusting one's own thinking flies in the face of the ability to use some level of reason that can assist one through the trials and tribulations of life. As a group, the thinking crowd relies less on the opinions of others, programs, or organizations to tell them how to think or behave. This is not to say that those who pride themselves on their intellect do not rely on others or programs for help when needed. They do. But the reliance is often limited, and they can tell stories of how they extracted themselves from problems by the way they reflected on things.

To some traditional observers, the critical thinking crowd appears dangerously arrogant and self-centered. They perceive hubris, and see non-reliance on others as fertile ground for clients deluding themselves into a severe relapse.

This gap persists to this day.

WHAT ELSE IS GOING ON?

Traditional addiction counseling has felt an element of discomfort with the notion of the intellectual. To many in the traditional camp, intellectual thinking conjures up bookish academics who wander their hallowed halls in far-away universities and are out of touch with the real world. They are perceived to generate ideas that are unworkable in theory and unrealistic in practice. Part of that stance arises from the belief that one cannot truly learn about addiction from textbooks, let alone apply such knowledge to how life really is on the streets.

Certainly people cannot learn and grow exclusively from books. Yet, a strong belief that has always existed in the recovery community is that one has to have lived through an addiction in order to really understand it. To this day, no one has put forth evidence that indicates significantly better understanding by those who lived through an addiction as opposed to those who have not (Buelow & Buelow, 1998).

This point of contention creates much of the mistrust between the camps. Those who have lived through an addiction often berate professionals and their credentials. One reason for criticism leveled at academia may be that some recovering people have felt the sting of the pompous academic put-down and believe if the intellectuals can zing people so can they.

On the other hand, many academically trained people have their own set of prejudices that add fuel to the fires of mistrust. For example, there are academics who flaunt their credentials to the so-called uneducated. These people are blatantly arrogant and let the other side know that they are smarter and more expert by virtue of their educational credentials. They make it known that they are not to be questioned by lay people, and that anyone in their care should follow their instructions with no questions asked.

This state of affairs can only lead to resentment on both sides. Stereotyping (a critical thinking flaw) often follows the resentment, and it all feeds the beast of mistrust. Once the mistrust is in place, communication slows or stops and then pernicious thinking takes over.

This mistrust is manifested by other, deep-seated elements within the clash.

DIGGING DEEPER INTO THIS MISTRUST

There is another point of contention between the intellectuals and traditional addiction counseling. It is the mistrust between personal experience given through testimony, which is viewed as immediate, understandable, and emotionally moving, and scientific reasoning, which is seen as distant, obscure, and aloof.

The traditional side cries, "They can't understand what they haven't lived," while the intellectual side cries, "You have a lousy research design and you use unsubstantiated data." Those who utter such phrases usually represent the extremes of both sides. As such they are often blind to other points of view, and believe they know exactly how things ought to be. Extreme ends of any spectrum will tell other factions how to live. Then clashing is inevitable, and that does nothing to advance our field.

IS THERE ROOM FOR NEGOTIATION?

Of the positions just mentioned, which is right?

Well, the answer to that question may not be simple. Arguing who is right usually leads to critical thinking mistakes, and fuels more ugly displays of personal favoritism. The better question may be is there room for dialogue?

Much more often than not, there is room for dialogue. One way to start an interchange is to use critical thinking principles such as reflecting before coming to a conclusion. Yes, this recommendation even includes those who identify themselves as critical thinkers.

A true dialogue requires courage. A large part of this interchange consists of questioning all your assumptions about the subject and generating reasoned alternative views (Taleff, 2000). This close examination includes your personal experience, your most cherished beliefs, and scientific facts. If the examined material makes it through the heat of close inspection, then it probably has a good foundation, and will be quite useful to you. If it doesn't, burn it.

CHAPTER SUMMARY

- Critical thinking is all about discovery (internal and external).
- Critical thinking consists of a set of tools to make those discoveries.
- Passion and critical thinking go hand in hand.
- Critical thinking is far from boring.
- Critical thinking is thinking about thinking.
- Think well and get better clinical, supervisory, administrative, and personal results.

- There are points of contention between the traditional addiction field and critical thinking. The traditional side tells you not to trust your thinking- because it will get you into trouble. The other side tells you to develop your thinking. The traditional side says you can't understand addiction by reading books. The other side says academic education is up to the task. The traditional side says follow a program philosophy to recovery whereas the other says follow science and evidence.
- There is generally room for dialogue and scrutiny despite varying positions.
- The heat of honest examination will often lead to better ideas.

CHAPTER TWO

Characteristics of the Critical Thinking Professional

We now need to define critical thinking beyond what was stated in Chapter 1. We will then outline the qualities of a first-rate critical thinker. Once these are established, we can move on to more ways you can apply this material to the addiction field.

Recall that our major focus is to encourage addiction professionals to instill elements of critical thinking into their daily work. Doing that, they will be able to detect and avoid many illogical thinking ruts that cause problems in treatment and programs. Such skills will also help prevent them from falling blindly into fallacies promoted by other professionals and literature.

Yet, old beliefs that have been ingrained in people over the years require many new learning experiences before they can be replaced (Halpern, 1998). The reward in addiction counseling is the ability to give clients the best distortion-free therapy possible. Clarity of thought, combined with an empathic stance, can make for a highly competent counselor and a smoothly running program.

It is time to balance the more traditional addiction counseling strategies with well-formed thought. For years the focus of many addiction approaches has been on the emotional, that is, "getting things out," or venting feelings. Critical thinking does not oppose the emotional element of therapy. Far from it. But now it is time to integrate *all* the functions of human capacity into a cohesive whole. That includes the thinking part of us. For too long, thinking and its benefits have been overshadowed in addiction treatment. While it remains so, we cannot provide the full symmetry of being human to the art and science of counseling.

A SHORT RECAP: GAINS TO BE HAD BY COUPLING ADDICTION COUNSELING AND CRITICAL THINKING

In the first chapter, we explored some reasons to include critical thinking in the addiction field. We need to highlight them and add a few more. One outstanding reason is that solid clinical decisions need to be based on solid reasoning skills (Gambrill, 1990). Sadly, many counselors do not realize how their errors of thinking (either hidden or unacknowledged) influence poor decision-making skills and lead to costly mistakes.

Carlson (1995) conducted a small survey to determine if there was any attention given to the reasoning processes of professionals. He found no literature that discussed evaluating the validity of information by professionals. Transferring this finding to the addiction field, I recently decided to take a small critical thinking survey. I examined twenty-five current books on counseling, treatment research, and ideas in the addiction field. Not one addressed counselor reasoning or critical thinking. Older addiction-oriented books also never mentioned critical thinking. A multi-billion-dollar business such as the addiction field leaving out instruction on how best to think creates a huge gap in our accountability and competence. Hence, one more reason for a book of this type.

A SELECTION OF DEFINITIONS

There doesn't seem to be one clear-cut definition of critical thinking (Angelo, 1995; Halonen, 1995). But that does not mean there are no definitions. There are numerous definitions and some are quite pertinent to our subject.

For example, Kurfiss (1988) indicates that critical thinking is exploring with a purpose. That purpose is trying to understand the real aim of a statement or argument. All assumptions we make, read, or hear about are open to question. Within this particular definition, alternative views are earnestly persued and examined in order to arrive at a reasoned, unbiased conclusion.

Paul (1993) defines critical thinking as those thought processes that are disciplined, self-directed, and display mastery of intellectual skills. It is thinking about thinking, as well as improving the thinking process, making it clearer, more accurate, and defensible.

This may be a good time to say that good critical thinking is not about attacking someone or some idea. Attacking is nasty and is an example of uncritical thinking. Rather, critical thinking is carefully weighing an idea or belief for its value and validity. "Critical" comes from the Greek word krinein, which means to place under judgment (Christian, 1977). So, although critical thinking means looking long and hard at arguments, it is not meant to attack another position.

Moore and Parker (1995) defined critical thinking as, "the careful, deliberate determination of whether we should accept, reject, or suspend judgment about a claim—and of the degree of confidence with which we accept or reject it" (p. 4). A claim is a statement that is either true or false. Generally, claims have some value, and, as anyone who has read the addiction literature can attest, we do make a lot of claims, all of which need scrutiny to examine their worth.

The Moore and Parker definition is very similar to Ennis's (1989) definition; McPeak (1981) adds the important element of reflective skepticism to the mix.

The authors of these and many other books and articles are quick to point out that there are no simple methods by which we can decide when to accept a claim. This process requires the use of many skills, including the ability to listen to and read carefully the claims someone makes. It also requires the ability to judge the worth of the arguments we encounter, while we look for hidden agendas that can determine various claims.

To illustrate, many in the addiction field accept at face value certain claims about the nature of addiction and the nature of clients. Acceptance too often comes without first considering the consequences of what a certain viewpoint does to their thinking, not to mention the actions those thoughts will lead to. One such consequence is labeling a client as resistant, when in fact such labeling can just as easily be the result of the poor thinking of a counselor (Taleff, 2000). These issues will be addressed more specifically later in the book, but a brief example is in order here.

Years ago when I was a clinical supervisor, I noted that both novice and experienced therapists tended to adhere to a notion that all clients referred to a program were in a state of denial. In the assessment portion of treatment, if the client didn't admit to certain behaviors, this was assumed to be clear evidence of denial. This assumption was built on a generalization, true to some degree and false to some degree, that addicts lie (Taleff, 1997). What was rarely thought to be a possible reason for the reluctance of a client to answer certain questions was the bad timing of those questions. Clients could have been in various stages of change, or perhaps they had not yet built up trust in the assessor. Fear, shame, or some other legitimate reason was an equally viable alternative to the denial presumption (Taleff, 1997).

In this circumstance, clients were (and still are) considered "guilty" before they even uttered a word. Little credence was given to the idea that a clearer understanding of the client could only result from a bias-free evaluation. A client's uncooperative attitude was not meant to be used to support some irrational belief of the assessor.

This example highlights the point that traditional and even newer forms of treatment have drifted into a pattern that is sometimes routine and automatic. If you have the opportunity to visit different addiction programs, you can see this process in operation. Across the country, programs often use these same philosophies, assessment practices, and strategies. Critical thinking is not encouraged and thus many myths are perpetuated.

A consequence of traditional philosophies is to force clients to think in selected ways and adopt certain phrases and platitudes. An important component of the agenda of this book is to abandon the idea of forcing our clients to think in preordained ways, and instead teach them *how* to think. That process starts with counselors and administrators.

I don't wish to be hard on those who think in the fashion just noted. It's natural for the mind to form patterns and reduce new ideas to the familiar (Dorner, 1989). However, the ideas laid out in this book rub against the grain of the familiar. To change a style of thinking is uncomfortable. It is unnatural for humans to constantly rethink their established systems, routines, and habits that have solidified over the years.

To rethink a point or claim can be downright threatening (Paul, 1993). When people feel threatened by views that are different from their own, there is a tendency to protect their threatened views, and narrow their vision by attending only to supporting viewpoints. Add to this mix those individuals who would tempt us back into the unthinking fold with slick, simplistic messages that proclaim some unfounded truth, and you get fertile ground for many prejudices that promote distorted thinking.

PROPERTIES OF CRITICAL THINKERS

Now that we have reviewed some definitions of critical thinking, we need to address a few characteristics of the critical thinker.

Sustaining these qualities creates a critical thinking spirit (Passmore, 1967) of curiosity and good judgment, which, arguably, are some of the better qualities of human nature (Raymo, 1998).

This spirit, in turn, sustains and improves critical thinking over time, but will not guarantee results unless it is constantly used. Paul (1993) has outlined a number of these characteristics that I have adapted for addiction professionals.

The first set of qualities includes the elements of humility, integrity, perseverance, and self-discipline. These traits foster and encourage intellectual fitness and an active mind. For example, critical thinking addiction counselors and administrators present their ideas in a modest manner. Through their investigations and experience, they do not declare that they have found some new truth in addiction science. Rather, they note that they have only added some piece of the puzzle to the pressing questions of addiction. The better critical thinkers do not look down their noses at people who disagree with them. They have integrity and are basically unassuming, honest, and upright, aware that being a good thinker does not mean being superior to others (Youngson, 1998).

Critical thinkers in the addiction field seek the best possible answers to difficult and thorny questions. They weigh new evidence against favored beliefs and can recognize fallacies in their thinking, detaching their own beliefs from the process of thoughtful evaluation (Stanovich, 2002).

Their persistence is demonstrated by quality time spent in libraries, or on the web, searching for literature to strengthen an argument or to bring evidence against one. Some are tenacious in the pursuit of an intriguing thought. They will sink their teeth into a delicious idea and will not let go until they have processed that idea to the fullest. They hang on until they, and trusted colleagues, are satisfied that they have reached a firm conclusion.

Critical thinkers are disciplined in their professional lives—not that their lives are stilted or rigid. Far from it. These individuals are passionate about their work. That passion provides them with an internal motivation to complete projects and examine new material and research (Pellegrino, 1995). All this does not make them perfect. They have their shortcomings like anyone else, but more than others, they work on their professional and personal development.

Another important quality of critical thinkers in the addiction field is that they can distinguish among different elements of their own thought processes. One such element is the purpose of their clinical questions. For example, they ask themselves questions such as, Where is a certain line of thought taking me? What is to be gained by this thinking? Is what I am thinking best for my client? Is what I am thinking best for my program? Moreover, they can identify a particular view of things, as well as provide relevant data to solve an issue (Pellegrino, 1995). For instance, critical thinking counselors can tell if they are using a disease model of counseling with a client, or an analytic, cognitive, or motivational enhancement one. In addition, they can tell you why they are utilizing a certain model at a certain time. Good critical thinkers can closely examine the research they are using in a particular instance. In this frame of reference, they can discern from which category of literature they have taken their information and are aware of the implications and consequences of their conclusions and assumptions.

Many in the addiction field do not have this level of thinking sophistication, nor can they step back and see a problem in a larger context. Such individuals are not mindful of the assumptions they make about treatment or administrative programming and often find themselves caught blindly in certain conclusions. For example, they will utilize a form of treatment that may not work for a particular client, but be unable to explain to their supervisor or themselves why their selection of treatment is not working. This can have serious consequences for those around them and especially for their clients.

Another important quality of critical thinkers in the field is that they are constantly assessing themselves to seek out strengths and weaknesses so as to improve their skills (Estling, 2002). They rarely rest on their past accomplishments. Such "resting" stifles professional development and makes them unreceptive to fresh ideas or innovations in addiction treatment. Sometimes this condition can even lead to *odium scholasticum* (Bauer, 2001), which is an attitude of smugness and hubris often exhibited by certain personalities and academics. You can observe this smugness when these individuals are confronted with theories or ideas that do not meet with their approval. They often dismiss such ideas outright through the use of belittling statements.

On the other hand, critically thinking and self-assessing addiction professionals are aware of their limitations as well as their abilities. They strive to improve those parts of themselves that need it but are not cocky about what they do well. They are never satisfied with the mediocre. They want to be good, if not the best, at what they do. Behind this drive to improve, you will often find the best interests of their clients as the driving force.

Another quality of critically thinking addiction professionals is that they are generally courageous. They do not shy away from an injustice they observe in their program or in the field at large. Such compelling honesty can place these people in the thick of a good debate.

A strong trait of these thinkers is their awareness of the many ways thinking can be distorted, misleading, prejudiced, or otherwise defective. This sensitivity to distortion adds to their passionate, well-reasoned responses and explanations of difficult arguments and clinical conditions.

KEEP THESE POINTS IN THE BACK OF YOUR MIND

A good way to end this chapter is to note some thinking flaws that permeate our age. Paul (1993) examines several erroneous points held by the public about thinking. The ideas are presented with a short rejoinder, and the application to addiction professionals is left to the reader.

- The idea: Many people believe that every person's opinion should be respected no matter how poorly supported. The rejoinder: Respect doesn't mean you think an opinion is right, just that you show some consideration for it. More importantly, the right to hold a belief does not guarantee its truth, or that it is as valid as other opinions. Some ideas are better than others and all beliefs and ideas are subject to critical examination (Mole, 2002).

- The idea: Users of language correctly use every word they employ. The rejoinder: Sadly, many people do not have a command of their language and can only vaguely convey ideas and thoughts. For example, many clients who first enter treatment seldom use clear speech because of residual drugs in their system or fogged thinking from those drugs.
- The idea: There are no widely utilized intellectual standards. The rejoinder: Of course there are widely used standards! They are called the principles of science.
- The idea: What were thought to be intellectual standards are often just a reflection of biases based on gender, culture, or a period in history. The rejoinder: There may be some truth to this claim; however, the spirit of critical thinking has the impetus to explore such issues, and may well be the means to continue a rigorous questioning of our rational standards.

CHAPTER SUMMARY

- The goal of critical thinking is to give your clients your best thinking.
- Critical thinking definitions include the following: (1) exploring with a purpose, (2) understanding that all assumptions are open to question, (3) pursuing alternatives, (4) "thinking about thinking," and (5) disciplined, self-directed, careful deliberation about whether one should accept a claim.
- The properties of critically thinking addiction counselors include: (1) modesty, integrity, perseverance, and self-discipline; (2) using perspective in their thinking; (3) a constant, honest assessment accompanied by improvement (which includes keeping any tendency to haughtiness in check); and (4) courage.

- Respect is difficult to bestow on certain lines of thought.
- Intellectual standards of thought and discovery do exist, despite the doubt cast by some.
- The ambiguous use of language.
- We are, in part, products of our biology, culture, and time.

CHAPTER THREE

Poor Thinking in Addiction Work: From the Individual to the Field

The last chapter described the positive human elements of critical thinking. In this chapter we survey the opposite: What drives poor thinking? The chapter attempts to paint a clinical picture of poor thinking from the individual counselor on up to administration.

Poor thinking might be regarded as the simple reverse of critical thinking. But it is more than that. Many characteristics of poor thinking have a special style all their own. They are also more encompassing than the fallacies we will examine in later chapters. The purpose here is to help recognize behavior that detracts from critical thinking and not fall prey to such traps. We will examine about a dozen such factors.

OVERCOMMITMENT TO IDEOLOGY

Although we all admire dedication to principles or beliefs, there are times when such dedication can become both limiting and all-consuming. This type of poor thinking is called an *overcommitment to an ideology* (Bandman & Bandman, 1988). It can be seen in some people's excessive commitment to religious beliefs or political principles, which do not allow any new ideas to enter their minds (Shermer, 2001).

Overcommitment is also found in the counseling field. Here it is referred to as *attribution creep* (Duncan, Hubble, & Miller, 1997). That is, counselors may begin to perceive clients through the lens of a preferred counselor theory rather than an objective lens. Because of the attribution creep, counselors may not understand clients as people, but rather as elements of a theory such as the disease model, various cognitive models, and the moral model, among others.

Counselors will sometimes persist in maintaining certain beliefs about clients in lieu of critical thinking arguments. This may be due in part to other colleagues and administrators in the same program who support a certain counseling orientation. Some addiction professionals become so committed to certain theories that the commitment outweighs ideas generated by the research data. Once convinced of a point of view, these same counselors and administrators will only attend to information that confirms that point of view and no other (Kowit, 2004; Levy, 1997; Snyder & Thomsen, 1988; Wright, 1994).

Once overcommitment and confirmation are established, zealousness is not far behind. Under this spell, individuals either refuse to listen to counterarguments (a closed mind) or simply cannot understand or accept alternative explanations. Either way, nothing that contradicts their belief system is allowed in their minds.

Clinically, this stance has extraordinarily dangerous implications in that a particular form of therapy that has no valid research foundation may be used time and again. Or administrators may use unwarranted business practices with a long commitment history that border on or are downright unethical.

BEHAVIOR IN THE FACE OF COMPLEXITY

A characteristic of some addiction counselors is their reliance on one-liners and catchphrases to explain addiction (Taleff, 1997). These are umbrella statements, which, as the statement implies, cover a lot of behavior in a single sentence (Bandman & Bandman, 1988). Although often well intended, such platitudes cannot account for the complexity of addiction dynamics. Said more formally, monological analysis does not solve multilogical problems (Paul, 1993). Or, as the physiologist Szent-Gyougyi stated, for every complex problem there is a simple conclusion that is incorrect (Calvin, 2002).

The one-liner is intended to keep things simple for the client. It comes, in part, from our limited human ability to process a lot of information at one time. So we resort to shortcuts that allow us to process it more rapidly and make the complex seem simple (Levy, 1997).

Let's use the complexity of addiction as an illustration. Addiction research findings will often contradict one another. This can be unsettling, to say the least. Sometimes, to adjust to this situation, counselors and administrators retreat into simplistic explanations. Why? One answer is that simple reasons are easy to understand and have the feel of certainty about them. Another answer is that many of us dislike wading into the muddy waters of conflicting research data. That disturbs our perception of an easy-to-understand world. In response to the insecurity some addiction professionals may use thinking patterns that are uncritical but comfortable.

A possible consequence of the safe and sure route is the loss of curiosity. Accepting the simple answer, one remains satisfied with a limited amount of information. Once that occurs, there is a strong tendency to avoid asking tough questions. Although non-critical counselors and administrators may indeed ask questions, sometimes those questions are not thoughtful and can sometimes come out in a defensive tone (e.g., What do you mean by that?), or have a distinct attacking tone (e.g., I had a client who tried Moderation Management and relapsed. How do you explain that?).

Tough questions, on the other hand, make one stop and think. To answer such questions requires a good deal of reading and research. Without such questions, our minds become stagnant and our field stops growing.

BEHAVIOR TAINTED WITH FALSE PRIDE

Addiction counselors are fond of saying that their clients deny having an addiction. They believe that clients' pride won't allow them to admit that they have a problem. So, clients begin to build a rationalization system to support their pride. This may be true of some people with an addiction, but certainly not true for all (Taleff, 1997). Yet, any counselor who has attended staff meetings cannot help but see that certain professionals are driven by the same malady-false pride.

False pride and its close cousin, vanity, are funny things. On one hand, they make us feel better about ourselves. They give us a sense of authority, if not power, especially if they come in the guise of status and professional advancement. On the other hand, these feelings are really based on a bogus opinion of ourselves.

For false pride to thrive there has to be a mix of self-deception and self-inflation constantly at work. We tend to deceive and overrate ourselves, from thinking we are more skillful in our jobs and other activities to believing we are more honest than we really are (Pinker, 2002). These overrated abilities, no matter how you slice it, are a deception and lead us to bad thinking. They make addiction professionals think they know more than they do, and that they are making better clinical decisions and judgments than they really are.

According to Adler (1927/1954), some of the more classic false pride behaviors include:

- Always behaving in ways in which you can plainly see that you are right and others are wrong
- Belittling others (or bodies of literature) in order to make yourself feel superior
- A constant and noticeable presence of hostility
- Shifting responsibility for any mistakes onto others.

One more attribute of false pride is an overconfidence in one's abilities and clinical assumptions. This mindset discourages the search for disconfirming data of any kind (Gambrill, 1990) and is fertile ground for the growth of unsubstantiated dogma.

Note that we are outlining the behavior of false pride, not the true level of pride we should rightfully feel with the completion of a difficult task. One might even argue that with true pride comes a certain level of modesty. As we saw in the last chapter, humility goes hand in hand with critical thinking.

ORATORICAL BEHAVIOR

Oratory is that which is spoken. It can be corrupted by the poor thinking that is sometimes found in addiction authors and educators. Their style utilizes a splash of the pride just mentioned, and the oratory is usually peppered with preachy words and attitude. You may have encountered these types of individuals. Their sole concern with ideas is to preach their own version with no interest in those of others (Estling, 2002).

When authors and educators put ideas out to the public they stake their reputations on those ideas. Once out in the open, these ideas are difficult to change. A major reason for this difficulty is pride. We become associated with the ideas we profess and the positions we take. We think that if our views are attacked or criticized, so are we. Because some of us believe our status is based on what we say and write, the thought of being wrong is closely associated with humiliation and any residue of false pride will not tolerate that. In addition, pride tends to distort our ability to think well, such that many fine thinkers go into a reactionary posture, defending and attacking anyone who criticizes them or their ideas. All of this is the antithesis of critical thinking.

Oratorical behavior may come naturally to us. According to Gazzaniga (2005), we humans are a storytelling species, and there may have evolved some mindless gut-level criteria that make us prefer one story over another. It is not a far stretch to assume that if a certain story feels right (has a gut-level resonance) then this evolutionary preference gets caught up in the human propensity to judge things based solely on these mindless criteria. That is, if it feels right, it has to be true. However, if that is the only criterion driving a clinical or administrative decision, a number of problems ensue.

Another uncritical oratorical behavior is that some writings and presentations in the addiction field rarely give adequate evidence to justify their conclusions. Key ideas are not thought through. Essentially, what we have is empty rhetoric, or a lot of emotion-laden talk, personal experience, and little substance.

Yet, rhetoric or oratory is what persuades people through the use of powerful words, verbal techniques, and even more powerful displays of sentiment (Bowell & Kemp, 2002). It seems to me that those educators or workshop leaders who resort to these practices enjoy hearing themselves talk. Often, they have hidden agendas. One important agenda includes mesmerizing an audience in order to get listeners to buy into a certain line of thought or dogma. The real name for this behavior is *conversion.*

Behind these displays of oratory lies the drive for power and prestige. The orations rely on simplistic beliefs, cajolery, and, at times, prejudices. These speakers will frame their presentations with imperatives that have overtones of a mission to accomplish or a destiny to fulfill. They are generally skeptical of reason or science. And there is that unmistakable air of haughtiness about it all.

In order not to be taken in by this behavior, you need to be skeptical. Question the aims of what is being put forth. Allow yourself to feel the presented emotion, to experience its pull. But then, balance the emotional with the rational and you won't end up a victim of unsubstantiated ideas.

POOR THINKING BEHAVIOR IN ADDICTION PROGRAMS

In addiction treatment programs many supervisors and administrators do not encourage their clinicians to visit a library to read the latest journals and books in the field. Without such visits, counselors are not exposed to the latest ideas in clinical practice, and so they often rely on outdated techniques. Feedback and creative interchange between supervisor and counselor or counselor and counselor then stagnate, to the detriment of the client, not to mention the professionals.

Because of a number of day-to-day program constraints (e.g., lack of time, understaffing), there is little opportunity to actively debate, reason, and bring forth new ideas on emerging issues in the field. Counselors are not encouraged to sit and deliberate issues in an open forum. Much more emphasis is placed on administrative issues such as keeping the client population high or getting paperwork completed before the end of another hectic day. If there are inservice programs or workshops, they often come in the prepackaged, non-researched variety where information is given and little debate or questioning is encouraged.

A mistake adminstrators and counselors make is confusing the simple recall of information with true thought. Victims of this error are chock full of incomplete data and biased information. Often the information is of the unconnected but impact type. It is usually inserted at strategic points to impress clients or staff.

When pressed to explain the accuracy of their fragmented information, these administrators and counselors often resort to personal experience or state something to the effect of, "I read it in a book (that was not based on research) so it must be true."

Facts certainly are used in this reasoning process, but good reasoning is much more than reporting facts. The critically thinking individual knows what is more correct and why. Genuine knowledge is that which is not only more correct, but the critical thinking individual who states it knows why it is so. These individuals can give an in-depth analysis of how their information is indeed correct.

Another behavioral flaw in treatment programs is the misuse of the intellect. Here non-critical thinking clouds issues and arguments. Uncritical thought is furthered by adding a particular bias to a certain stance, or it is used to defend a narrow-minded interest. All clinicians, both novice and experienced, have some biases (Arnoult & Anderson, 1988; Garb & Boyle, 2003), but when they are not kept in check, the result can be the cultivation of manipulation—the very thing the addiction field believes most of its clients personify.

Some addiction professionals have been observed using shrewdness over intelligence, cunning over clear, and imprecision over accuracy. These are the "oily talkers," the crafty and arrogant. They often lack high intellectual standards, but attempt to pass themselves off as intelligent.

An additional type of uncritical thinking found in some treatment programs involves parroting platitudes and saying "the right thing." Such platitudes seem at times to be force fed to clients, who in turn are rewarded and considered to be in true recovery. Free and critical thinking is often thought to be heretical to the standing philosophical view of a program. In addition, critical thinking is often thought of as a form of rationalization or intellectualization fostered by the client who wishes to get away with something.

One last point needs to be mentioned again, concerning thinking problems within addiction programs. There are flaws inherent in certain systems. That is, certain systems tend to confuse subjective opinions with reasoned judgment. Many addiction professionals believe in the correctness of their "gut" feeling. Recent evidence indicates that people vastly overestimate their ability to judge simply by watching someone's behavior (Carlson, 1995).

Feelings are a means to determine if we like something or not. They should not be used to evaluate the authenticity of an idea, theory, event, or behavior (Levy, 1997).

So when counselors judge an event in counseling using only their feelings, they do not realize that their feelings are often biased. Objective methods to evaluate clients provide more reliable answers than gut feelings (Carlson, 1995; Dawes, 1994). Without the ability to use critical judgment, there is a tendency to resort to less valid methods of assessing situations such as the charisma of a subject, the familiarity of a source, or the trappings of pseudoscience (Carlson, 1995). More will be said about this in later chapters.

POOR THINKING IN ADDICTION STUDIES EDUCATION

A recent survey (Taleff, 2003) indicated that of a sample of 1028 higher education courses surveyed in addiction studies programs across the country, not one mentioned critical thinking by name. A study of recent national examinations for counselor certification reveals not a single question concerning critical thinking. In addition, an examination of nearly twenty syllabi from the community college level to the graduate level noted only one syllabus that even mentioned critical thinking.

Observing addiction studies education (college, workshops, online) for nearly two decades, I see that a certain standard predominates. Many students are schooled in memorization of facts and simple rhetoric. They are rarely taught how to think, or how to explore the evidence and logic behind certain conclusions presented in a class or in a text. In response to this style of teaching, many students simply feed back what has been fed them, often simply to get by in a course or receive a better grade.

Paul (1993) notes certain characteristics of non-critical thinking that are found in this lower-order style of teaching. For example, many classrooms are heavy with slogans and catchphrases. This display confuses repeating watchwords with high-level thinking.

Another example is the confusion between an uncritical opinion, and one that is arrived at critically. The trouble usually begins when educators indicate that any opinion is of equal value to any other. Such positions diminish intellectual standards. Some statements that reflect such unsubstantiated sentiments take the form of, "I'm a feelings type person." This is sometimes meant to mean that an internal feeling tone colors all of the feeling type's perceptions. But, what sense does that mean when dispensing a diagnosis to a client? Or, "I have a right to my own opinion." You indeed have such a right, but realize that your opinion may be inaccurate and you may be called on it. Simply put, some opinions have more value than others because there is more critical thought behind them. When addiction professionals muster such weighted opinions, program and personal development take a step forward.

The last issue in addiction education to be discussed is the human need for a sense of certainty. Many students will tell you that one of the reasons they go to college is to get answers. This is definitely one element of education, but an equally if not more important one is challenging one's beliefs. This means grappling with tough questions. Good courses and good teachers do that; they make students think and question their values and previous positions. If, as this book has been at pains to point out, the idea survives the challenge of hard questioning, then it is worth retaining.

Many people in many cultures will plainly exhibit discomfort when what they have been taught to believe becomes uncertain. When times of uncertainty do arise, many resort to uncritical thinking, which they hope will give a sense of solidity to their worldview even if it isn't supported by facts. This is illustrated by the many powerful convictions people retain in the face of contrary evidence.

The need for certainty leads to unjustified systematic errors (Carlson, 1995). For example, there is a belief that almost all individuals addicted to mood-altering chemicals require some form of treatment or a self-help group in order to get better. However, the data are clear that most people in this country quit an addiction on their own (Prochaska, Norcross, & DiClemente, 1994). Yet, when those who recover this way encounter those who think treatment or self-help groups are required, the latter often resort to systematic thinking errors such as, "They weren't really alcoholics in the first place," or "Sooner or later they'll relapse." By the use of such "logic," some people can retain their sense of certainly that recovery occurs only in line with their thinking. That, unfortunately, does nothing to advance critical thinking, and has all to do with prejudice.

In a sample of students, as well as seasoned professionals, it is likely that most would not be able to outline the basic elements of an argument, let alone describe a few common thinking fallacies.

The sad part about all this is that many addiction professionals believe they think very well just because they graduated from college or have many years of experience. If asked, most would say that their thinking is good and level-headed. Yet, thinking errors consistently appear in print and in person. These thinking errors clearly indicate the need for the inclusion of critical thinking courses and workshops into the education of addiction professionals.

CHAPTER SUMMARY

- Counselors and administrators can become so committed to certain beliefs that they will reject alternative explanations outright.
- One factor that contributes to poor thinking is the counselor's inability to grasp complex ideas and instead resort to simple explanations.
- Another is attribution creep or the perception of clients through the lens of a preferred theory rather than objectively.
- Conduct based on false pride is sure to bias all thought.
- Oratorical behavior based on pride and with a goal of conversion is certain to result in biased thinking.
- Not encouraging critical thinking or research time in treatment programs and relying on simple or emotionally loaded thought will affect vital clinical decisions.
- Providing addiction studies education without a thorough analysis of the content or without mention of critical thinking principles will perpetuate bias.

CHAPTER FOUR

Evaluating Your Critical Thinking Abilities

If you've read this far, you are up to your neck in critical thinking and nothing bad has happened. So, you are now asked to take two little tests to assess the personal state of your thinking. They are inserted here because you might appreciate your answers a little better now than if they were presented at the beginning of the book. They can also serve as a baseline for how you will grow.

THE FIRST TEST

Answer the following questions honestly and, if you like, retake the test for comparison after you finish the book.

1. How do I know the ideas I have about addiction treatment and theory are good ones?
2. If I were pressed to explain a trustworthy addiction theory could I do it well?
3. How do I know my clinical and administrative ideas are reasonable and rational?
4. Do I defend my clinical and theoretical claims with sound information, or do I become defensive and lash out with emotional displays?
5. Have I tested my ideas recently to see if they are accurate and clear?

6. If I have not tested my ideas, how can I be sure they are accurate and clear?
7. Can I ponder addiction ideas in an absorbed manner, or do I think in a superficial fashion?
8. Do I assume I am right all the time, or can I entertain opposing ideas?
9. Do I know how to question myself and test my ideas?
10. Do I know the addiction terrain around me, or am I simply following someone else's path?

WHERE ARE YOU?

The next brief test asks you to locate yourself—honestly—on the scale provided (Table 4.1). Read through the various levels and return to the level that best describes you right now. As with the test above, consider coming back to this assessment following the completion of this book.

Elder and Paul (1997) developed this six-stage critical thinking scale, which includes elements of a similar scale developed by Kurfiss (1988). It has been adapted for this book.

TABLE 4.1 Stages of Critical Thinking

STAGE 1: The Unreflective Thinker

- Individuals at this level are largely unaware of thinking and how it is involved in all forms of human endeavors.
- Hence, they fail to recognize how the lack of thinking contributes to the problems in their lives.
- Prejudices and misconceptions undermine the quality of thought at this stage.
- There is a tendency to see knowledge as simply collecting information or data.
- Information, to them, is either correct or incorrect.
- They think of their beliefs as true.
- They often become confused and irate if ideas appear in perplexing forms.

(continued)

TABLE 4.1 ***(Continued)***

- They unreflectively take in many absurd thoughts because those around them do the same. (This uncritical analysis paves the way for future thinking problems.)

STAGE 2: The Challenged Thinker

- These individuals begin to recognize that ideas and doctrines can and will conflict.
- They have begun to see that knowledge and thinking are complex.
- They have begun to see that ideas have many sides.
- They have started to become aware of how their thinking affects their lives.
- They have begun to be aware that high-quality thinking requires deliberate reflective thinking about thinking.
- They have begun to recognize that their thinking is often flawed, but still cannot identify many of the flaws.
- They can begin to recognize the role of self-deception in their lives.
- They may still deceive themselves into believing that their thinking is better than it actually is, even following some exposure to critical thinking education.
- They still lack the intellectual humility that can block awareness of their own ignorance.

STAGE 3: The Beginning Thinker

- Here individuals recognize the flaws of their thinking and begin to take steps to rectify the problems.
- They lack a systematic plan for improving their thinking. Yet, they see the importance of maturing into a critical thinker. They begin to take up the challenge of thinking seriously.
- They become more aware of the role of concepts, assumptions, inferences, and other points of view.
- They begin to recognize standards of thinking such as clarity, accuracy, precision, relevance, logic, breadth, depth, etc.
- They recognize that they often misuse words.
- They begin to recognize egocentric thinking in themselves and others (i.e., thinking without giving due consideration to the rights and needs of others).
- They recognize that good arguments are supported by good reasons.

(continued)

TABLE 4.1 Stages of Critical Thinking *(Continued)*

STAGE 3: The Beginning Thinker *(cont'd)*

- They are beginning to develop a degree of intellectual confidence that they can think well, and they persevere by not giving up if problems become difficult.
- They begin to struggle with ways to express questions clearly when addressing a problem, and take deliberate steps into that which is unfamiliar or initially thought to be wrong.

STAGE 4: The Practicing Thinker

- Here individuals are more aware that their thinking needs to be improved. They now begin to develop corrective plans.
- They can now critique their own thinking plans.
- They have enough skill to monitor their own thoughts, and become more passionately invested in understanding.
- They can effectively clarify the strengths and weaknesses in their thinking.
- Their thinking is now driven by questions that require accurate information and purposeful answers.
- They begin to see the "moves" one makes in thinking well.
- They begin to see connections between varying subjects.

STAGE 5: The Advanced Thinker

- Here individuals have established good thinking habits that are paying off.
- They can analyze their thinking and have significant and deep insight into themselves.
- They generally have good control over egocentric thinking.
- They continually strive to be fair minded, but sometimes lapse into one-sided reasoning.
- They have a deep understanding of how thinking plays a pivotal role in their lives.
- They have a higher degree of intellectual humility.

STAGE 6: The Master Thinker

- At this level, individuals have taken charge of their thinking.
- They continually monitor, revise, and reconsider strategies to improve their thinking.

(continued)

TABLE 4.1 *(Continued)*

- They are engaged in ongoing self-assessment.
- They have a high degree of control over their egocentric tendencies.
- They are conscious of how their minds work.
- They are highly integrated, powerful, logical, fair-minded, self-correcting, and free.
- They capture the interplay of rationality, caring, and responsibility.

Now that you have your personal responses and the information obtained in the previous chapters, we can proceed to the nuts and bolts of critical thinking.

CHAPTER SUMMARY

Two short self-tests were administered to assess some of your personal strengths and limitations in the realm of critical thinking. How did you do? As you read on, keep your results in mind.

A reminder: After you finish this book, consider coming back to these pages to retake the tests. If you feel so inclined, consider retaking the test every now and then to compare your results over time, and note if your level of critical thinking has changed.

CHAPTER FIVE

Learning the Basics of Critical Thinking

You are now pretty much swimming in the waters of critical thinking and you need to know that this chapter gets a little technical here and there. Don't worry; there is nothing in it you can't handle.

THE BEDROCK OF CRITICAL THINKING

This book rests on a pivotal concept called *inference* (Hughes, 2000). It refers to a special relationship between different thoughts. Inference differs from merely thinking and from causal explanation (Fisher, 2001). When we are merely thinking, thoughts come to us, one after another, with no particular link. When we use causal thinking, we simply connect ideas by inserting a word or phrase between the ideas like "because" or "that's why." No forethought or reasons are given to the connection, just a causal "because." Some people believe these meandering ideas constitute real critical thought. But they have no particular structure or goal. They feel comfortable, however, and on occasion serve us well, as in personal tastes or appreciation of art. Yet, with no structure or goal, all sorts of thinking problems can arise.

Inference, on the other hand, asks, even demands, that one thought is supported, justified, or reasonably linked to another. The greater the strength between ideas, the better the overall thought. How this is done and what problems get in the way of good inferences are the bulk of what is to come.

A FEW TERMS TO KNOW

People and programs in the addiction field are forever advancing their ideas. These ideas come in the form of statements, called *claims,* and are either true or false (Dauer, 1989; Moore & Parker, 1995). A claim is something you want people to believe (Booth, Colomb, & Williams, 1995). For example, advertisements for some addiction programs make the claim, "a program that gets to the core issue," or "one of the nation's twenty best programs," or "you can gain personal empowerment and wholeness with our trusted staff and facility." Nice claims, but how true are they?

An important critical thinking approach to test such claims is to ask a few simple questions. For example, questions directed at the first statement above might be: How does one determine a core issue? Once it is determined, how does one go about assessing its truth? What does "gets to" mean?

As to the second claim, some critical questions might include: What are the established criteria for the top twenty best programs in the country? Who sets those standards? Does top twenty mean success with clients, or does it mean something else?

As to the third statement, some questions might be: Don't all programs want to empower one and make one whole? If so, what's so different about how your program goes about empowering versus how another program might empower? How does one measure empowerment? What is your yardstick?

The field will continue to make claims, but critical thinkers will need to ask how true such claims are. A few simple but tough questions are a step in the right direction.

A nice summary of simple but tough questions comes from Booth and colleagues (1995). The questions are accompanied by the beginnings of responses. These examples are adapted for our purposes.

Your question	The desired response
What is your point?	I claim that . . .
How reliable is your claim?	My evidence is . . .
Have you any reservations about the evidence?	Yes, and they are . . .
Then just how strong is your claim?	Its limits include . . .

When addiction professionals make claims about a theory or a program, they are usually trying to support a significant point. In the examples above, the significant point is the quality of a treatment program. That was the issue in all those examples. And, an *issue* is the focus of a contention, argument, or debate. One would not usually make claims for such issues if they were not in dispute or up for review (Moore & Parker, 1995). Because all issues in addiction studies are up for review, we have to make claims about them. Sometimes those claims are less than factual. People might deliberately try to confuse issues in order to call attention away from claims they cannot prove or do not want to deal with. Sometimes they will try to make you believe they have proved a point, when in fact they haven't. That's why critical thinking in the addiction field is so important. It helps you separate the wheat from the chaff.

We just used the word *factual.* It is important that we establish clearly what it means. Confusion often arises when we mistake opinions for facts. *Facts* are claims that are true or have good evidence or justification. *Opinions* are those beliefs and attitudes that someone accepts as true (Moore & Parker, 1995). Whether someone believes in a claim or whether it is an actual fact are two different things. The job of a critical thinker is to ascertain the context in which a claim is made and then determine what the maker of the claim is up to besides just handing out information. The critical thinker needs to figure out the issue. So, were the program statements listed above facts or opinions?

When people in the field make claims for their ideas and programs, how do you decide whether to accept those claims? We indicated that one way is to ascertain if the claim is an opinion or a fact. If it is a fact, how, then, can it be proven to be true? This is where logic comes into play. *Logic* supports assertions with reasoning (Kurland, 1995). It takes us from one point to another in an assured and sensible manner. Logic is interested in the correctness of a claim and how well one inference follows another.

ARGUMENTS

Our discussion now brings us to the elements of *argument* or a set of claims. In good arguments there is always a main point or *conclusion* that is supported by *premises* (Hughes, 2000). Premises supply reasons, or facts, for accepting a conclusion (Hughes 2000;

Moore & Parker, 1995). Arguments are supposed to settle the trustworthiness of claims.

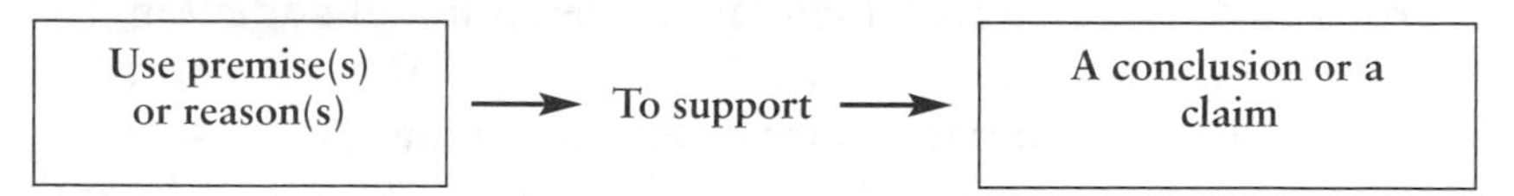

So, if a program makes a claim that you will "become whole" by attending a certain treatment center, you now have an argument. This particular argument has a principal conclusion (becoming whole) that needs to be supported by a set of premises. A critical thinker will ask to see those premises to determine if the principal conclusion is true. The critical thinker will also need to see clear definitions of terms used in any argument. Good thinkers do not stand for sloppy definitions that can obscure a claim.

One last important point: do not confuse the fine art of true arguing with the loud, screaming versions sometimes seen on TV, in movies, or, sadly, in some addiction programs. The type of arguments presented in this book never result in a physical exchange.

Fine Points of an Argument

So far, we have outlined the essential components of an argument, but there are a few other secondary process-oriented issues to address. The first is *clarity* (Moore & Parker, 1995). When you listen to an argument, the clarity of that argument means:

- an argument that is plainly defined
- an argument that is understandable
- an argument in which the presenter is not merely trying to win followers
- an argument in which there is ample evidence for a principal conclusion
- an argument that is free of ambiguous or vague statements or premises.

If an argument can have more than one meaning, or the meaning has not been made clear, then it is ambiguous. Ambiguity comes about when the speaker makes a poor choice of words to support the argument and/or when there is no clear conclusion. If an argument is vague, its meaning is inexact and imprecise (Moore & Parker, 1995). Examples of this ambiguity include the sweeping claim made in the addiction field that most members of our society have some form of addiction, or else enable those with an addiction. Such wide-ranging claims are meant to warn people of the extent of a problem. Yet, they water down a true definition of addiction.

These definitions are ambiguous and vague. Why? Because the more broad a definition the more people and things you have to include in it. That means differences disappear and everyone and everything is included. Such definitions become useless because they can no longer discriminate among their elements. Definitions by nature are designed to be specific.

The field of addiction counseling can't afford such ambiguity and vagueness. It demands clarity of thought, precision, and specificity. This is especially true when it comes to making a differential diagnosis for each client we see. In these cases, it is important to know exactly what the problem is and how, specifically, it is to be dealt with. The client needs to be on the receiving end of clear thinking.

We need to know whether the evidence for a claim is germane to the conclusion. This is called a *warrant* (Booth et al., 1995). For example, if someone is trying to make a point about biological elements of addiction, we expect biologically oriented evidence in the premises, not psychological ones. Someone who presents an addiction argument needs to keep the facts connected to the points and conclusions of the argument.

The last fine point of any argument has to do with the *qualification* of the conclusion (Booth et al., 1995). No fact or theory in the social sciences will have a universal application. All our facts are limited to certain segments of a population, region, or time. A treatment that works in one segment of society may not work in another. So, despite all the discoveries made about addiction science these days, there are no certainties about any one discovery. Times change, people change, and more discoveries will be made in this field. Sooner or later, much of the information we have today will go out of date, as has happened in the past. Critical thinkers know how to keep a sharp eye on material they receive as to its inherent possibilities and/or limitations.

Specific Addiction Counseling Arguments

Consider that a stated diagnosis, the interpretation of behavior, and the choice of a particular treatment approach for a client are arguments. In the case of a diagnosis, you base your conclusion on inferences, reasons, a few warrants, and some qualifications. If you do all of this well, these items will lead you to a confident diagnosis or conclusion. The same applies to interpretations and the selection of a particular treatment for a certain client.

If you have doubts about the process that leads to these clinical findings, consider asking the following set of questions (adapted from Fisher, 2001).

- What are my reasons for giving the diagnosis?
- Are such reasons based on the best available facts?
- Where is the evidence for the treatment approach I chose?
- How strong was my inference to an interpretation I put forth?
- Are my warrants justified for my interpretations?
- Have I considered any limitations to a diagnosis I made?
- Have I considered any limitations to an interpretation I made?
- Have I considered any limitations to a treatment selection I made?

TYPES OF ARGUMENTS

We have examined the inside of an argument. Now let's take a look at some varieties of arguments. They range from the simple to the complex (Hughes, 2000). Every argument must have a conclusion and at least one premise. These items must be connected with an implicit or explicit word such as "therefore," "hence," or something of that nature. For instance, the *simple argument* has one premise (P) and one conclusion (C). An example might be "I note a consistent pattern of uncontrolled drinking with my client" (P), and hence conclude "he has a drinking problem (C).

Other types of arguments are called *complex arguments*. They have two or more related premises and one conclusion (Hughes, 2000). In such cases, all of the premises are needed to make a claim. For instance:

Every addiction counselor has the ethical obligation to keep a client's record confidential (P1). Beverly is an addiction counselor

(P2). Therefore, Beverly has an ethical obligation to keep her client files confidential (C).

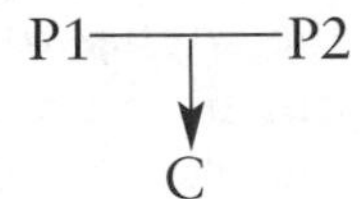

In another complex argument, we can have two or more premises, but each premise can stand alone and still lead to a conclusion. However, they make for a stronger argument together. This is called a *V argument* (Hughes, 2000). For example: George (a client) feels the need to use cocaine almost every day (P1).

Frank is experiencing troubles at his place of employment due to his abuse of cocaine (P2). Therefore, George has a cocaine problem (C).

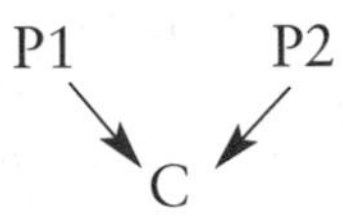

There are other complex argument types. Generally they vary from the basic types just shown by adding one premise onto another. So, if you understand the three types of arguments just outlined, you have a good handle on this process.

NEAR ARGUMENTS

Sometime you may find yourself encountering things that look like arguments but are really not. There are two types of these so-called near arguments: *reports of arguments* and *explanations* (Hughes, 2000). Reports of arguments do just what they say they do. They report that an argument was conducted in a certain way. For example, "Bob has openly stated time and again, and in rather strong and colorful language, that he refuses to attend a certain type of self-help group." This particular statement is like a photograph of a real argument. It details what decisions Bob has made and with what level of conviction. This report doesn't spell out a set of reasons. It just makes an observation.

The second near argument is the explanation. It can be confused with a real argument because they share a common vocabulary. For the most part an explanation attempts to show why or how something happened. For example, an addiction counselor can state that a client is ranting and raving because he's angry, or administrators are always thinking of costs because they are business people and really don't have a heart. This provides some answer to why or how something has occurred, but it doesn't indicate how correct the explanation really is. Although useful at times, such an explanation should not be confused with a true argument.

A FEW IDEAS TO CHALLENGE AMBIGUITY

It is sometimes difficult to tell when someone is making an argument. People complain, express opinions, observe, make allegations, tell stories, give examples, and so on (Hughes, 2000). So, let us finish this section with a short set of criteria for a sound argument, and a series of addiction-oriented questions to clarify ambiguous arguments. First, we examine the criteria for solid arguments.

There are three basic criteria a good argument must meet (Hughes, 2000).

1. Premises must be *acceptable.* That means they need to be true. If false, a premise cannot provide support for a conclusion.
2. Premises must be *relevant.* This means that they need to be related, correlated, and appropriate to the conclusion. Including premises from quantum physics or spirit guides isn't relevant to addiction arguments.
3. Premises must be *adequate.* Generally, those with a research base will be more than adequate to support a solid conclusion.

Next, we need to consult Socrates, and a method he developed to find the truth. It is a form of questioning called the *dialectic.* It discards unsound arguments and retains those that stand the test of scrutiny. In the dialectic, you essentially take a position and then question that position to assess if there are any contradictions or fallacies. If there are, you create a revised position and question it again. If it fails again, you revise it until you find something that withstands the questioning (Stewart & Blocker, 1982).

There are, of course, other questions that will shed light on ambiguous addiction-oriented arguments. Bates (1995) and Moore and Parker (1995) supplied some overall ideas, which are adapted for this book. They are divided into two basic types of questions. First are those you need to ask in your everyday work. We just examined many of those types of questions in this and previous chapters.

The second set of questions was adapted from Carl Sagan (1996). He produced a questioning yardstick based on whether you could trust educational material (e.g., class, workshop, and reading material) to be useful or not. The yardstick was called a *Baloney Detection Kit.* However, for our purposes, and in honor of the addiction field, which likes to use the term "bullshit," it has been modified, with additional input from Allegretti and Frederick (1995), and renamed *the Bullshit Detection Kit.* It has two parts and the parameters are listed below

The Bullshit Detection Kit for Everyday Issues

- Ask yourself if the ideas (clinical, supervisory, administrative, books, and articles) you are exposed to every working day are clear.
- Ask yourself if the ideas you hear in supervision or in staff meetings are clear.
- In such meetings, is good evidence provided for clinical conclusions?
- Is the clinical evidence relevant?
- Could there be any qualifications that need to be made to evidence cited for a clinical claim?

The Bullshit Detection Kit for Educational Material (classes, workshops, and reading)

- Does the presenter stick to the issue or does he/she engage in fallacy-prone thinking?
- Does the presentation have a logical sequence?
- Does the presentation make a point/claim and then provide support for it?
- Can you restate the point (write it in your own words) and indicate the research and or argument support?
- Have the prime arguments or hypotheses been tested?
- Is there weight given to competing hypotheses, and are such hypotheses eliminated if they fail to explain the findings in question?

- Does the presentation reach a conclusion?
- Are there points of summary and closure?
- Is the argument complete?
- Is the addiction material dispensed in an emotional, knee-jerk, response-seeking manner? That is, does it try to appeal to the feelings of the audience with superficial and unrelated information?
- Does the presenter drone on about how important the subject at hand is without getting to the real issue?
- Does the presenter obscure the point of an argument, or does he/she address it directly?

Apply these sets of questions to a familiar or a new reading, class, or workshop. Weigh your answers carefully to discern quality from bullshit.

TWO MAJOR TYPES OF ARGUMENTS: DEDUCTION AND INDUCTION

Now that you have the argument fundamentals and guidelines in hand, we need to focus on two time-honored types of argument. This section also notes how these important argument types apply to the addiction professional.

Deduction

This argument form has been traditionally considered the pure form of reasoning (Cannavo, 1998). It can be referred to as theory-driven or top-down reasoning (Levy, 1997), and is also known as the type of argument designed to provide certainty (Bandman & Bandman, 1988).

The deductive argument is simple. It consists of at least two premises (reasons, statements) that are leading toward a conclusion. So, if your premises are true, the conclusion that follows will also be true. For example, in order to be classified as an alcoholic, one has to meet certain DSM* criteria (Premise 1). Richard meets the DSM alcoholic criteria (Premise 2). Therefore, Richard is an alcoholic (Conclusion).

**Diagnostic and Statistical Manual*, 1994.

As long as the two premises are valid, the conclusion will be valid. In the lingo of logic, if these conditions are met, the conclusion follows *necessarily* from the premises (Hurley, 1997). Deduction says, "I expect this would happen if . . ." (Ray, 2000). This type of reasoning allows the thinker to make assumptions from general statements and beliefs to specific conclusions (Kurland, 1995; Magee, 1998). In the example above, we started with a general assumption (alcoholic criteria) and ended up with a specific conclusion (Richard is an alcoholic). The premise-premise-conclusion reasoning is called a *syllogism* (Kurland, 1995).

This type of thinking takes place in staff meetings, supervisory sessions, and especially when a counselor is trying to make a diagnosis (Bensley, 1998). For the most part, the conclusions drawn from this line of reasoning are fine. However, there can be problems.

First, the premises have to be true. If they are not, or if they are ambiguous, the conclusion will be false or tainted. Second, most discussions in clinical meetings are not as clear as the example we gave. They can be intermixed with extraneous side issues, such as emotional displays and thinking errors that are often assumed to be accurate. A dubious conclusion can then be taken back to the client. For example: Premise 1: Alcoholics are always in denial. Premise 2: Richard is an alcoholic. Conclusion: Therefore Richard is in denial.

The problem with this syllogism is the basic premise. All alcoholics are *not* in denial (Miller & Rollnick, 1991; Taleff, 1997), thus making the conclusion false in this particular case. So, even though a conclusion sounds convincing, if the first premise is incorrect, the clinician who came to this conclusion will have an inaccurate perception of Richard, who may not be in denial. Such a perception will prompt a misrepresentation and subsequent clinical troubles.

One more detail about deductions: the conclusions pretty much say the same thing that has been stated in the premises. This has been referred to as *circular reasoning,* which doesn't do more than repeat a claim hidden in the premises. So, the major limitation of a deduction is that it does not provide any new conclusions (Cannavo, 1998).

The caveat, then, for using deductive reasoning is to make sure your premises are accurate and understand that by relying too heavily on this argument form, you may not have really advanced new information. That brings us to the next traditional form of thinking.

Induction

Deductive arguments can guarantee the truth of a conclusion but inductive arguments cannot. Rather, they give you high or low probabilities of truths (Hughes, 2000), and always have levels of uncertainty (Bandman & Bandman, 1988). This process is sometimes referred to as *data-driven* or *bottom-up processing* (Levy, 1997). Here we step into the field of scientific reasoning and the ability to make fresh discoveries.

In a nutshell, scientific reasoning is about classifying observed objects or behaviors, providing a description of them, and offering satisfying explanations of our observations (Magee, 1998; Youngson, 1998). Induction is at the core of this reasoning; it represents most of the everyday reasoning we all do. It is practical, investigative, and advances knowledge (Cannavo, 1998). In this argument form, we ask, "I wonder what would happen if . . .? (Ray, 2000).

Induction is the process of leading into (Honer & Hunt, 1968). We observe and collect data, and then perform inductions (lead into) generalized statements that may lead to general laws (Vivian, 1968).

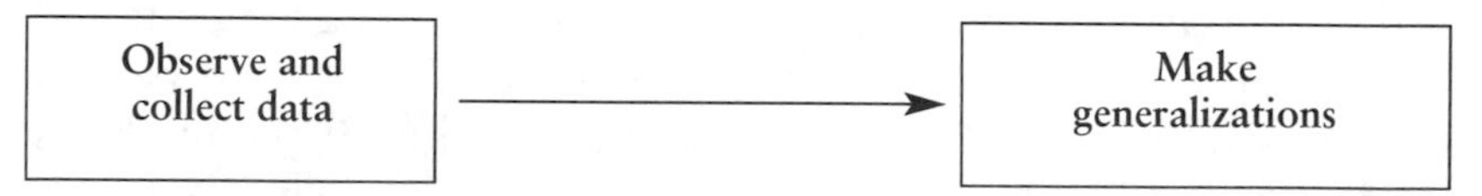

For example, if all the alcoholics addiction counselors have ever known were in denial, counselors would be tempted to generalize that all alcoholics are in denial.

Sounds good, but the drawback is that inductive arguments are less certain than deductive arguments (Cannavo, 1998). Case in point: What would happen to the denial belief if one day an addiction counselor ran into an alcoholic who wasn't in denial? In such a case, the counselor would have to modify that generalization to fit the new facts. As in the deductive argument, induction relies on precise and accurate evidence (Vivian, 1968). Where deductive reasoning allows you to make specific conclusions from general statements, induction extends arguments the other way: from the particular to the general (Hughes, 2000; Kurland, 1995).

A generalization arrived at through induction is a conclusion. That conclusion can be called a *hypothesis*. A hypothesis can be utterly false or very probably true before it is tested (Dewdney, 1997; Hospers, 1953). For example, check any old book on addiction counseling to see how many "truths" have held up over time. A number of those "truths" did not fare well. Why? Because sooner or later researchers tested those claims to see how they held up and they failed the test. That brings us to science.

THE SCIENTIFIC METHOD

Induction can only take us so far in our search for quality addiction information. If we theorize or question, however, we can provide direction for our inquiries. Because our generalization, conclusion, or hypothesis can be wrong, we add theorizing or questioning to induction and arrive at a higher form of argument called the *scientific method* (Fraenkel & Wallen, 2000).

Science makes new discoveries, creates new theories, and refines our knowledge (Fraenkel & Wallen, 2000). The acid test of any idea (e.g., addiction theory) must be the evidence for and against the idea (Ehrlich, 2001): that is, its ability to be tested and shown to be false. Facts need to have the quality of being testable. And, if you can't show something to be false, it cannot be tested and therefore is outside the realm of science. The method behind science is little more than a way to check reality. If the methods used to test a hypothesis are properly applied, then a built-in safeguard against error has been created (Dewdney, 1997).

In scientific thinking, we combine deduction and induction to form a new syllogism called the *hypothetical syllogism* (Honer & Hunt, 1968). That's a fancy way of saying, "If so and so, then so and so." For example, if I claim alcoholism stems from personal insecurity, then I have created a rough hypothesis—if so and so (personal insecurity), then so and so (alcoholism). Many professional authors and clinicians make such statements. That is, they hypontesize. But, as valid as such statements sound, how true are they? Here is where we need to put such hypotheses under the microscope of research.

This comes under the umbrella of *hypnothetico-deductive* research (Bensley, 1998; Hayes, 2000). This high-sounding phrase simply means testing a hypothesis. A good hypothesis tries both to explain and make predictions about theories and observations (Wynn & Wiggins, 2001). A solid test or experiment will determine if a theory or an explanation of a set of observations is true or not. If all goes well, then you can make deductions from your test results. In chart form, it looks like this:

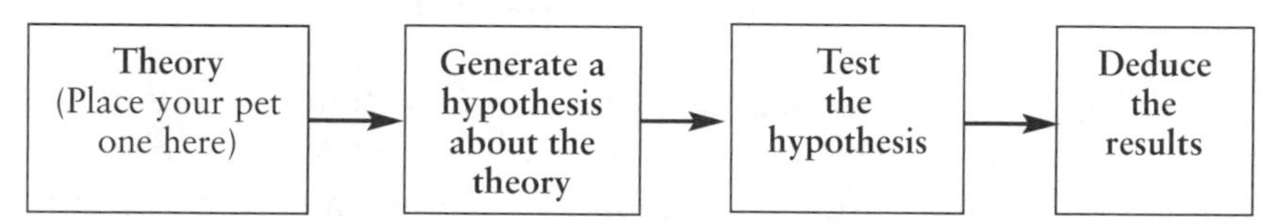

You need to remember one last thing about this process. Once the results are determined, you will need to feed them back into the theory to see if it was accurate or predicted what it said it would. This feedback process often modifies the original theory. That new theory now has to be tested again. This constant retesting and refining of theory is the essence of science. Said another way, the scientific method contains four essential and repeating steps (Bordens & Abbott, 1996).

- Observe a phenomenon
- Form a tentative explanation of cause and effect (theory)
- Observe and experiment (or both) to rule out alternative explanations (test)
- Refine and retest the explanation

This retesting process gets us closer to facts and better theories. That means we can then deduce facts for clients in our clinical work with more confidence than we could through other forms of arguments. Such theories often account for the most information with the fewest assumptions. Technically, this is called *Occam's razor* after the fourteenth century philosopher who proposed it (Bronowski, 1978; Tavris & Wade, 1995).

With this method, how would we use our earlier example that states that alcoholism stems from personal insecurity? We first would create a hypothesis about some element of personal insecurity (say shyness). Then we would survey and statistically test it on a sample of alcoholics, find the results, and feed them back to the original theory. As always, we would need to retest and reconfigure the theory. After a few rounds of this process, we would either have a high level of confidence that insecurity contributes to alcoholism theory or not.

Of all the arguments noted in this chapter, the scientific method is by far the most honest and reliable.

ONE SMALL CAUTION

To date, the problem with addiction research is that nothing in the field has ever been termed absolute law. Unlike the hard sciences, addiction dynamics are extraordinarily complex and at times elusive. There will always be variables that intrude on our conclusions (Friedlander, 1995). Variables constantly change, and so will our established conclusions. Do not fault the process of research, however. We can still get close to some pretty good conclusions. That's the beauty of the scientific method and the reason critically thinking addiction counselors need to understand it.

Knowing what this chapter offers will help protect you from misleading claims and make you a better thinker. Your clients, stakeholders, and colleagues will thank you for it.

CHAPTER SUMMARY

- Inference is a special relationship between different thoughts.
- The basic elements of an argument include at least one premise and one conclusion, and are connected by a form of the word "therefore." In other words, start with a set of premises, formulate a conclusion, and you have an argument.
- Arguments range from the simple to the complex.
- A statement that is either true or false is a claim.
- Claims are used to support larger issues.
- Facts are claims with good evidence, whereas opinions are beliefs.
- To navigate through various claims requires the use of logic.
- Good arguments will be clear, have relevant evidence (warrants), and will note their limitations (qualification).

- Near arguments simply report on or explain certain arguments.
- Use these criteria (acceptance, relevance, adequacy), and set of questions provided to clear up ambiguity, along with good questions and a detection kit.
- There are two classic forms of argument. One is called deduction and requires at least two premises that lead to a conclusion. This process is called a syllogism. Deduction allows you to make specific conclusions from general statements. The second is called induction, where you observe behavior and induce (generalize) theories. Any conclusions drawn are called hypotheses. Induction allows you to make general conclusions from specific statements. Within the realm of induction is the scientific method. The process is called hypnothetico-deductive research.
- *Occam's razor:* keep your assumptions to a minimum while explaining the most evidence and you've probably got yourself a good theory.

CHAPTER SIX

What Drives Bad Thinking?

Let's explore what drives poor thinking a little more. Back in Chapter 1, we examined a few motivations. There are many more, and you might appreciate this discussion a little better now that you have a good command of critical thinking fundamentals.

Addiction professionals continue to make thinking errors despite all our education and scientific understanding. For instance, addiction counselors try to figure out what clients are doing and why. Supervisors do the same thing with counselors, and administrators generally try to figure out ways to make ends meet. Sometimes these addiction professionals draw conclusions that defy all logic. So the question becomes this: What is behind this bad thinking? There is no simple answer; many things propel faulty thinking.

AN OVERVIEW OF REASONS WE THINK BADLY

We are all susceptible to bad thinking, no matter how bright or educated we are. One reason is that our minds are not always well organized (Raymo, 1998). For another, we are a species that relentlessly reflects on itself (Blackburn, 1999) and in that process a fairly universal problem occurs. Our perceptions distort the world (Roth, 1990). The reasons for this distortion are varied and complex.

Some authors have taken a stab at this complex problem and have come up with some interesting ideas (Beck, 1999). This chapter uses some of Beck's ideas, coupled with others, but there are many more reasons that drive us to think badly than the list provides. Reading and considering these drives will deepen your understanding of why addiction professionals, and other people as well, do what they do. Knowing the "why" may help you avoid your own bad thinking.

BASIC DRIVES

Our ancient ancestors often lived under a state of threat. They did not always have the luxury of thinking a situation through—especially when something wanted them for dinner (Wright, 1994). Such situations required a quick and impulsive response. This "react, don't think" process helped us survive as a species, and even though we are less often thought of as dinner these days, that type of thinking has remained with us. We still tend to react to threatening situations without reflective thought. Thus, under a perceived threat, some people unthinkingly strike out and say and do things they may not have done if they had given the situation a little more thought (Beck, 1999).

Parallel to the "fight or flight process" are our other natural propensities. For instance, we are all heavily influenced by our experiences. Experiences color our perceptions of the world and often make it difficult to envision something outside of ourselves clearly (Youngson, 1998). Another natural propensity is that we are all born to magical thinking (thinking I made something happen when I didn't), not to reason (Alcock, 1996). Morris (1999) asks, "What is stronger in human life, rationality or irrationality?" His answer is a no-contest vote for irrationality. Inherent in the irrational are uncontrolled emotions that exercise more power than intellect does. It is no secret that strong emotion can overwhelm rational judgment (Perkins, 2002). Add to this imagination gone amuck, and these forces can make us do irrational things.

This doesn't make emotions and imagination, in and of themselves, bad. Without them, you and I would not have our passions and causes. However, faulty thinking arises when emotions and imagination have no guidance.

Natural propensities and the more survival side of evolutional thought fall under the category of *primal thinking* (Beck, 1999). Here we think strictly in terms of what is good for us or bad for us—egocentric and very selfish thinking. Not much critical thought occurs at this level. What thinking we do at this point is crude and unbalanced. It is mostly non-analytical, concrete, and action oriented (Alcock, 1996). In this state of mind, we are prone to make outrageous demands and to accept simple if not inaccurate explanations. Hence, we are much more likely to make thinking errors. We are a frail thinking species (Murray, Schwartz, & Lichter, 2001).

In line with primal thinking is *emotional cognition* (Burns, 1980), which gives the illusion of real thinking (Alcock, 1996). For example, let's say you firmly believe in some addiction theory (e.g., disease, moral, habit, etc). You have used it in your practice for years. One day you attend a workshop and the presenter takes one pot shot after another at your pet theory. Soon you find yourself becoming upset. You begin to challenge the presenter and your emotions rise even more. You may soon get to a point where no amount of evidence or argument will influence you. You have achieved a "hot thought" (Carlson, 1995). You believe that what you feel must be true.

Sometimes our clients do the same thing. For example, if they have no self-confidence and believe that they are shy or stupid, then to them, it is so. Such emotionally loaded beliefs can and will distort quality thinking.

DRIVES ORIGINATING FROM ROUTINE

There is evidence that people harbor thinking routine shortcuts called *heuristics* (Carlson, 1995). We need these shortcuts because they streamline and organize the way we go about our personal and professional lives. Yet, shortcuts can often turn into ruts. Examples of heuristic ruts are excessive dependence on slogans and platitudes. When they are used as broad guidelines, there is no problem. Some are actually quite good, but we can get lazy and rely on them too much. For example, using slogans to resolve complex problems. As soon as we do that, we start missing the complexity of life, and begin to pigeonhole things and people without much thought. It is this type of reliance on heuristics that can lead to systematic errors in reasoning.

Even ideas and theories we hold dear can lead to dogmatism, and insensitivity (Solomon, 1999). It's not the ideas that lead to dogma and insensitivity, but the inflexible grip they can sometimes have on us that leads to problems. There is no question that theories are critical to understanding the world around us. It is only when they become ossified in our minds that they become dangerous. Once ideas and theories turn to dogma, we close our minds (Wynn & Wiggins, 2001). Once a mind turns into concrete, how can it possibly think well?

This hardened thinking is just a few steps away from fundamentalism. Fundamentalism is an extreme form of narrowed thinking and intolerance of alternative ideas. Be it religious, political, concerned with addiction counseling, or otherwise, it is extremely dogmatic and immature. It blunts solid intellectual thinking and interferes with problem solving (Morse, 2001). Addiction professionals who drift into fundamentalism will not be able to think straight or solve problems well. As humans, we have always tried to find something stable in which to believe. Yet, our propensity to turn stability into dogma has brought centuries of tragedy to the world (Magee, 1998).

Another element of the routine is Langer's (1989) concept of *mindlessness*. Here individuals become trapped in rigid mindsets created by habit and daily repetition. Driving to work, getting your coffee, seeing the same slate of clients and the same colleagues, having lunch, doing the same basic paperwork—well, you get the drift. In terms of clinical work, this mindlessness contributes to dulled decision making. Soon most all your clients look the same (Taleff, 1997) and you lose the ability to recognize novel distinctions in the people you observe (Moldoveanu & Langer, 2002). This will cause problems for any client who is under the care of such a mindless counselor. If the situation is not corrected, clinical rigidity soon follows. That is, unique situations will be perceived based on frozen previous knowledge. Clinically, that means clients will receive a biased assessment and therefore a biased treatment plan.

DRIVES ORIGINATING FROM THE HUMAN MIND ITSELF

Closely related to routine is another set of reasons humans think badly. In this mix is the human propensity to jump to conclusions (Pigliucci, 2003), the need to explain things (Scruton, 1996;

Youngson, 1998), and the tendency to reach some level of certainty (Murray et al., 2001). To illustrate: listen to people talk to one another following a local or international news event (e.g., earthquake, flood, accident, etc). Some will conclude that the event happened because of divine intervention, negative karma, "it was bound to happen," or some other glib explanation. The same sort of discussion can occur among addiction professionals sitting around a staff table.

The need to explain brings out our propensity to think in relationships or patterns (Shermer, 1997), or, as Charpak and Broch (2004) and Peat (2003) note, the propensity of the human mind to create theories and explanations. This relationship-making process is important to us in that it provides good general ways to cope with life. The patterns we form about ourselves and the world around us help us avoid starting from scratch each time we encounter similar events (Pinker, 1997). Without these patterns, we could never learn from our mistakes because we would constantly be relearning everything we do.

Yet, helpful as these patterns are, they are also simplified views of an infinitely complex world (Roth, 1990). We tend to see things around us the way we expect them to be, not necessarily the way they are. Often, our preconceived patterns do not fit different situations. In order to understand such differences, people try to force their own personal set of patterns (generalizations) onto those different circumstances, and sooner or later this will produce poor thinking. Essentially, when a pattern of events occurs, it triggers a need to understand; however, we often come up with an explanation robotically (Halpern, 2002).

A last facet of these mind-engendered drives comes from Allport (1954). He indicated that the human mind needs to think by using categories. If we didn't think in such a manner society would not run as smoothly as it does. By using categories and stereotypes, we can reduce the complexity of life into manageable bits. Our brains are constantly filtering out extraneous information so we can move along. However, this simplification comes at a price. That price is our tendency to prejudge people, places, and things by the very categories we have created. Imagine what an unhealthy dose of prejudgment can do to all the new clients you will encounter!

THE DRIVE ORIGINATING FROM "IT'S JUST TOO HARD"

Another reason many professionals do not think critically is that they often consider the language of science too difficult, arcane, and far removed from everyday forms of communication (Alcock, 2001). Scientific thinking requires effort (Beck, 1999). Moreover, the language of science is unintelligible to those not familiar with it. It is no wonder many clinical people shy away from it and turn to nonscientific reasoning that is more intrinsically appealing (Vyse, 1997).

One of the criticisms of scientific language heard within the addiction field is that science, especially addiction research, does not speak the same inviting or warm language as does counseling. Therefore, it is considered a distant if not alien tongue, not applicable to true human interaction. To be fair, part of this sentiment is accurate and part is not. Yes, some scientific addiction writing is obscure and badly stated. But a few poorly written research pieces should not condemn the entire enterprise of addiction research. You can certainly find clear writing in some research-oriented books or chapters in edited texts.

On the other hand, counseling gems can be found if you labor through difficult chapters. If you give up too soon or maintain a stance that such reading is too hard, you might never find those diamonds in the rough. Sometimes there is no magical technique to make things easy. You just have to work hard.

DREADED CHANGE

One last major reason that drives us to think badly comes from John Locke, the English philosopher, who noted it some 400 years ago. It is that new ideas and opinions are usually met with suspicion, and then opposition. Why? Well, one reason is that they are different (Hoffer, 1963). New ideas generally make us uncomfortable. As we stay with older ideas, our mindsets about those ideas become stronger and stronger. Part of the reason for that strengthening is that we select only those ideas that feel comfortable (Ruchlis, 1990). Once those thoughts become reified we find it difficult to get free of them and move on (Vos Savant, 1993). When an idea becomes *reified* it means that something that merely has a conceptual base has been turned into something that is considered concrete or actual (Levy, 1997).

All the ideas in addiction science are trying to best describe its complexity. The words we use in this explanation process not only describe but also evaluate (Levy, 1997), and much of evaluation in the addiction field has a tone of finality about it. Arriving at that finality is the reification process at work.

So, if you become over-familiar and overinvested with something, be it a particular approach to addiction treatment or broad-based addiction philosophy, it may become a trap. The trap is that you think you are an expert. Some experts might even consider themselves elevated to the status of unquestioned authority and are not likely to consider another point of view (Shekerjian, 1990). In essence, they become the reified establishment.

You can recognize a symptom of this state once other addiction professionals start to criticize the so-called authority's work or beliefs. He or she becomes defensive because we humans like things the way they are and become suspicious if not downright hostile when we have to endure change.

Under the threat of change, some people muster all the bad thinking they can in order to maintain the status quo. Observe it yourself. Addiction counselors, supervisors, and administrators will do it. Even whole factions within the addiction field will do it. To justify their aims, they will turn to different forms of rationalization and say something can't be done, or resort to the most egregious statement of all, "That's the way we (I) always do it." Treatment procedures, policies, and procedures become ingrained to the point of hardened tradition. Once this status is achieved, very few people even think to question those traditions. In the end, not many people are immune to the uncomfortable condition caused by change. Even critical thinkers experience it.

We humans try to reduce what is new and strange to what is old and familiar. In some cases, as we have said, these patterns of thinking can become ruts (Paul, 1993). Ruts have a feeling of safety and security about them, but they don't allow for growth. They encourage staying the same. Staying the same is not an attitude we want for our clients or our field. How we recognize and avoid such ruts is the subject of the next few chapters.

CHAPTER SUMMARY

- All humans are prone to think badly. There are a number of things that drive us to do that.
- One drive starts in the more primitive part of our brain that overreacts to threats, irrationality, and hot cognitions.
- Another drive is routine and the propensity to rely too strongly on heuristics. Do this and you end up in a mindless rut.
- Another drive is the natural propensity for our minds to form categories. If allowed, these categories can grow into an inflexible state, and soon we begin to prejudge.
- There is the drive not to persevere, because the work, reading, or class, is too hard.
- Finally, we all shrink from change.

PART II

Fallacies and Final Thoughts

CHAPTER SEVEN

A Crash Course in Fallacies

The next set of chapters point out more of the rocks and undertows to avoid while swimming in critical thinking waters. We are going to spend a lot of time on these hazards, so, we first need to discuss what we mean by fallacies, and a distant cousin called mind tunnels, and why both doggedly stick to us.

Recall that decisions are based on all kinds of thinking. Some of that thinking is good, like the type that uses solid reasoning and evidence-based arguments. Some arguments are not so good, like those that resort to fallacies. But what are *fallacies?* They can be mistakes, omissions, faults, and false beliefs. Fallacies have everything to do with making arguments defective; they supply a wrong conclusion from a set of premises (Bandman & Bandman, 1988; Engel, 1976; Hurley, 1997). They lull us into the sleep of reason (Blackburn, 1999), and are difficult to change once they become established.

Fallacies masquerade as true when in reality they aren't (Browne & Keely, 2004). To fall prey to a fallacy is a surefire way to misconstrue the true nature of a client or the thoughts and feelings of other addiction professionals. They cannot change things for the better (Blackburn, 1999). Fallacies are pernicious and can occur at any stage of the reasoning process, from formulating premises, to establishing connections with those premises, to making inferences (Grigorenko & Lockery, 2002). Clients and treatment programs that are on the receiving end of fallacies face serious problems.

MIND TUNNELS

In the previous chapter, we noted how many people tend to follow a few favored ways of thinking because those ways feel comfortable and familiar, and even help us with day-to-day living. These favored thinking assumptions and patterns are known as *mind tunnels* (Piattelli-Palmarini, 1994). Yet, such thinking patterns may not lead us to what is true (Bandman & Bandman, 1988). They are not necessarily actual biases, but simple and inexact rules that serve to resolve certain classes of problems.

One reason we lean on mind tunnels so much is that the brain can only process a limited amount of information. Its nature is to automate in order to reduce cognitive loads (Perkins, 2002). So, instead of going through a host of complicated theorems, the brain uses crude rules of thumb (Pinker, 1997): these mind tunnels.

Although beneficial at times, mind tunnels cannot adequately answer a pivotal question. For example, when supervisors ask addiction counselors how they arrived at certain clinical decisions, let's say the choice of a certain treatment modality for a particular client, many counselors cannot articulate a clear answer to that question. That could be in part because counselors have relied, without examination, on inexact rules for years. Placed in the spotlight to explain themselves, they may well rely even more on these established mind tunnels, which did not answer the supervisor's question in the first place, and now turn out to be even more inadequate. If pressed to clarify, some counselors will resort to improvisation or justification (or another set of mind tunnels). A circular pattern of thinking occurs because these justifications turn out to rely on other pre-established mind tunnels. All this mental juggling is not conducive to quality clinical decision making. Administrative mind tunnels can take forms similar to the clinical ones, relying on inexact rules to assess pay increases, improve office space, or install safety equipment.

Remember that these established thinking routes are approximate or rough rules, often performed automatically, (Piattelli-Palmarini, 1994), that can shortcut deliberate thinking processes. Those who resort to these thinking shortcuts are not the people who are perplexed by problems. Due to their pre-established thinking routines, they seem to know exactly how to respond, and believe not only that their decisions are correct, but that their position is incontestable (Piattelli-Palmarini). In terms of the counseling process, this rigidity can create an array of problems in the therapeutic session.

THE TENACITY ELEMENT

Mind tunnels and overused fallacies are resistant to change. There are a number of reasons for this (Gambrill, 1990). One reason is their apparent strength. That strength comes from our core belief in them. We believe they have served us well; many of us can recall winning arguments using a certain mind tunnel or fallacy. This service in turn promotes a high level of confidence to continue to use them. Such perceived "merits" make us reluctant to give them up.

Then there is the longevity element. We have lived so long with our fallacies that they have become second nature to us. If you live with anything long enough you will have difficulty changing it. Moreover, when the way we think is challenged, we often feel personally attacked (Levy, 1997) and then most of us tend to dig our heels in and cling even more tightly to our thinking styles.

Then there is the smugness element. Many of us pride ourselves on the way we think and believe deeply that our thinking has served us well. Such pride increases resistance to any change.

Finally, in this list of tenacity elements is the avoidance of clutter. The thinking we do and the way we do it allows us to make sense of the world and do it in a fairly streamlined fashion. This style avoids the bother and mess of learning new styles of organizing our world. Things are figured out in a simple and efficient manner. Under such conditions, why change?

All these elements can combine to create a tenacious hold on our (often uncritical) style of thinking, to our detriment and that of our clients.

BROAD IDEAS TO AVOID MIND TUNNELS AND FALLACIES

There will be suggestions in the coming chapters on how to avoid specific fallacies. However, this section presents a few broad ideas on how to manage thoughts well. These simple but effective critical thinking suggestions can help you detect ambiguities, make reliable arguments, avoid confusion, and become aware of alternative possibilities (Blackburn, 1999). They are suggestions you can turn to over and over again. Without some kind of constant adjustment and tweaking, assumptions can lead to all kinds of errors and distortions in reasoning (Carlson, 1995).

So, how does one avoid falling into various fallacy and mind tunnel traps? The first step is to try to identify them. Fallacies are statements, and they rarely if ever hold up well to questions, especially the following questions (Browne & Keeley, 2004):

- What is the proof of a statement?
- Where is the evidence for the statement?
- Why would I want to believe the statement?
- How can I be sure the statement is true?

Once you get into the habit of asking these types of questions you will have a good defense against the many fallacies that follow.

Many fallacies confront critical thinkers, but you are not expected to learn them all. However, these chapters are organized in such a way as to give you a classification of fallacies with selected examples in each.

The fallacies that you will encounter in this book were primarily accumulated from a number of authors (Browne & Keeley, 2004; Engel, 1976; Fearnside & Holther, 1959; Hurley, 1997; Sutherland, 1994). A few other authors are also noted. The procedure was to take the fallacies and simply apply them to the addiction field. Depending on whose work you read, fallacies are classified differently. This book follows those formats put forth by Bandman and Bandman (1988), Gambrill (1990), and Gibbs and Gambrill (1996). Their classifications systems have a clinical orientation, which made it easier to translate the material into addiction-oriented issues.

ONE SMALL WARNING

Once you complete the following sections you may feel confident that you will be able to spot a fallacy easily. Don't fall into that trap. Don't think that just because you discovered a fallacy the conclusion under examination is automatically false. It still might be true. All you have uncovered is that one path to that conclusion is false. Other and more valid arguments could still prove the conclusion true (Fearnside, 1980). In other words, don't jump to conclusions. That is *not* critical thinking.

CHAPTER SUMMARY

- Fallacy—a defect in an argument
- Mind tunnel—a favored thinking assumption
- These uncritical thinking properties are tenacious due to our confidence in them, their longevity, their value and our pride in them, and the fact that they help avoid everyday clutter.
- Good methods to avoid fallacies and mind tunnels include recognition, vigilance, and the application of avoidance tips.
- Conclusions can still be true even if there is a fallacy in the reasoning.

CHAPTER EIGHT

Fallacies That Appeal to Authority and Irrelevant Fallacies

This chapter explores those fallacies steeped in authority (the so-called experts), and those that provide irrelevant information. The authority family of fallacies is covered first.

AUTHORITY FALLACIES

Somewhere in the addiction field, someone is always presenting a claim or argument based solely on authority. Such arguments can be found operating everywhere, including staff meetings, lunch conversations, and even in the ivied halls of addiction education. Driving this type of fallacy is the manipulation it exerts to make you believe what influential people want you to believe, not what is really true. If you find yourself so persuaded, without supportive data, problems await. The central weakness of authority-based fallacies is that they are not based on reputable research. Moreover, a number of overarching reasons drive these fallacies as we will see below. But, all of them are powered by the allure of authority.

The Direct Authority Appeal

The lure of authority comes in a number of forms. The direct authority appeal asks you to believe in the opinions of certain people because they consider themselves or are considered experts. These individuals often pass themselves off as such by their sheer audacity and overconfidence. Their appeal is their forceful manner and convincing language. Such people in our field maintain that their years of experience (and often that experience alone) qualify them to profess certain "facts" concerning addiction. They tout 20 or 30 years working in the field as their authority credential. To some extent this longevity appraisal is reasonable. Knowledgeable professionals generally have spent longer periods of time devoted to a subject than unknowledgeable ones, but time in the field alone is not sufficient to claim expertise (Sexton, Whiston, Bleuer, & Walz, 1997).

Some "expert" addiction professionals possess some kind of state or national certificate or license, and therein lies their lure. Many of our well-known spokespersons have an M.D., Ph.D., or other prestigious degree(s) after their names. In addition, many carry a title like director or president. All these credentials and titles cry out: authority figure.

Authorities also carry weight because of the books they write, or videos and DVDs they produce. Many people assume that those who can do these things, must know what they're talking about. Sometimes these "experts" don't have titles or haven't written any books. All they believe they need is personal experience with the problem. That is, they need only indicate that they are recovering themselves to carry the aura of authority.

Just because someone has a fancy title, a degree, or a past addiction; has written books; or narrates a set of DVDs doesn't mean that person has a corner on addiction facts. Such people have frequently turned out to be a lot of show with little evidence to shore up their "facts."

All of us have a tendency to buy into what authority figures say even if they don't supply supportive data. One reason is that in our youth we generally were taught to respect our elders and authority figures (Gambrill, 1990). As children, we took in all kinds of information solely based on authority (Moldoveanu & Langer, 2002). Tell children a pleasant myth and they will generally take it as the truth. People in our field sometimes pick up information via the same method. They are told something by an authority and they simply believe it. For much of its existence, the addiction field has overrelied on authorities. It seems mesmerized by certain "names."

As stated, time in the field or having a similar problem yourself is indeed useful. But on the other hand, this form of authority has its dangers because what was once purported to be a fact can be later dismissed due to the lack of research or to new research. This means that with the very best intentions, many authorities have professed false positive or false negative ideas. A false positive means accepting a wrong idea even though an authority supports it. A false negative means rejecting a good idea because an authority thinks it is dangerous or false when it is not.

We need to add the popularity factor to the authority allure. We have all seen pop psychology and addiction treatment methods come and go. It is in the coming part that many counselors can get caught up in the authority appeal. Here counselors tend to believe that because authorities are using a new pop addiction treatment, then they should too. The counselors who jump on the pop bandwagon often do so without thinking. Caught up in the rush, they can make bad clinical mistakes because the authorities they rely on have used little data to support their ideas. For example, it was once thought we all had some sort of an "inner child." However, no data exists to remotely support such a claim.

There is also the appeal to popular sentiment. Here, some authorities will use catchy terms and phrases in order to appeal to an audience. These terms include a host of stereotypical phrases intended to grab the emotional attention of the reader or workshop attendee. Once the emotional side is captured, the mind often unquestioningly and willingly follows.

You can see this overall authority effect in the advertisements of certain programs. For example, a few years ago the field got caught up in various dysfunctional family styles. A number of so-called authorities outlined colorful names and characteristics that were supposedly indicative of how family members responded to an active alcoholic. Counselors and lay people flocked to these family workshops and bought hordes of books on the subject. They did so because the concepts had a huge bandwagon effect. Yet, many years later no reliable data have ever been published to add substance to these characteristics. Critical thinking at the time would have revealed that catchy phrases and emotional presentations do little to advance the quality of our field.

You should not be left with the notion that all authority figures are suspicious characters. Many people in our field have and deserve fine reputations. They are to be admired as true authority figures. However, they achieved their status the hard way: they did the research. Their reputations rest on the evidence they have been able to uncover and demonstrate.

So, in order to avoid falling into direct appeal to authority fallacies, here are a few ways to make a distinction between the authority-based arguments that have supportive research and those that do not (Gambrill, 1990).

- Note whether an authority cites references that support a claim. For example, if an authority claims that all people with alcoholism are from dysfunctional families, does that statement come from a set of research articles or merely from other authorities?
- Does an authority figure consistently use impressive but vague terms or emotionally loaded words to make a point? If so, be suspicious.
- Does an authority figure state a claim based mostly on his or her experience, credentials, or some popularity standard? If so, be suspicious.
- Does an authority figure cite straightforward research accounts, or just make obscure references to data? If it is the latter, again be suspicious.

With the first set of authority signs and warnings out of the way, let's move on to reasons to be cautious around other authority fallacies.

Appeals to Traditional or Folk Wisdom

This fallacy is not much different from the one we just left, but in this case the appeal is not to a person; it is to a doctrine or a thing called a *meme* (Brodie, 1996; Dawkins, 1978).

Let's first address what we mean by doctrines. They are some of the canons and dogmas of our field. For example, one canon that's been around for a long time is that alcoholics and drug addicts are manipulators and con artists and are not to be trusted. Faced with such doctrine, addiction counselors have been implored to confront clients in order to break through the denial-embedded manipulation.

These dogmas have been around for a long while and are considered revered wisdom, evoking a certain respect. Couple their presumed wisdom with their long life and you end up with pretty powerful doctrines. To those who accept them, such doctrines are "the way things are supposed to be done" in the addiction field, with no questions asked.

Many in our field indeed think questioning is not appropriate. However, once you fall into this doctrine fallacy, you will have problems (Gambrill, 1990) because much of this dogma and folk wisdom lacks a reliable foundation of research data. Unfortunately, this means that many addiction professionals are practicing counseling with a head full of authority-based biases.

The meme is a unit of information that influences thinking and events; those influenced thoughts, in turn, creates more copies of themselves (Blackmore, 2004; Dawkins, 1978). It is something like a gene but on a social level. Memes can be true or false, and they spread from mind to mind like a virus. They can enter your mind unbidden, become part of your programming, and influence your life without your realizing it (Brodie, 1996). Examples include generations of people being taken in by the lure of the drug culture with all its promises of feeling better and gaining insight just by taking drugs. Countless people were taken in by this meme and it significantly influenced their drinking and drug behavior for years. Another example of the addiction field meme can be found in treatment programs. This particular meme had counselors believing that a single treatment philosophy should be used with all clients. It spread and influenced programs such that all clients were treated in the same fashion, regardless of their individual differences.

Appeal to the Many

This fallacy is very similar to appeals to popular authority and folk wisdom. However, the *appeal to many* gains its strength from consensus: the belief that "everybody is doing it" so it is the right thing to do. Another name for this fallacy is the *bandwagon effect* (Gambrill, 1990). Now mix in some self-centered thinking, what the in-group is doing, a pinch of loyalty, blind faith, and made-up evidence, and this fallacy has extraordinarily strong appeal.

Staying true to something is laudable, but it can also get in the way of progress. For instance, there is a very strong feeling in our field that treatment centers should operate on a philosophy called a Minnesota Model approach, based on the thinking of a few authority figures years ago. In this approach, treatment is roughly conducted as follows: clients are confronted, required to take on the label of alcoholic or drug addict, taught to believe they have a disease, and regarded as being in denial and incapable of making sound decisions (Miller & Rollnick, 1991; Volpicelli & Szalavitz, 2000).

This model has been around for a long time and has gained legions of followers. When a new treatment program is started somewhere in the country, that program will generally follow this format. The likely reason is that very few people questioned this model, and accepted it outright, and thus, this approach has to be the thing to do.

The problem with accepting this model is that it can rule out programs with a different orientation, perhaps based more on current research.

Stories Equal Science

A slightly different fallacy, yet one very close to those we just examined, is *equating anecdotes with science.* Here the fallacy is not based on authority figures or the prevailing folk wisdom. Instead, authoritative stories are told to support certain claims. Essentially, a story or anecdote is used as scientific data.

The well-known client testimony is one example of equating story to science. Clients often report that program "x" saved their lives. This testimony is sometimes translated into a marketing ploy that tries to prove that program "x" is better than other programs. No other evidence is offered to support such a claim. Yet the testimony is taken as scientific evidence that program "x" is indeed a superior one.

If the same client had gone to program "y" it may have saved his/her life there as well, and the recovery story could just as well have been used by program "y." Moreover, a single testimonial is not sufficient to make superior program claims.

Stories rarely serve as scientific evidence. They are not designed to do that. The fallacy trap in this case is that one is led to believe that emotionally moving personal stories can and should be accepted as proof for a doctrine or meme. Yet as unkind as it may seem to say, a story needs corroborative evidence from other sources before it is to be believed.

SMART STRATEGIES TO ENGAGE AUTHORITY FALLACIES

Here are some more guidelines that can help you avoid falling into the various authority traps just listed.

- Take a long look at the evidence and arguments of any authority figure.
- The long look is especially critical if one authority figure disagrees with another.
- Be careful not to accept anything in our field at face value.
- For the more industrious, keep a track record of the experts. Survey their past performances and determine how well they score on a scale of reliable current research.
- When you encounter an authority, ask the all-important question, "Can you show me your data?".
- Does the authority represent a vested interest?
- Does the authority have the relevant expertise/training? (Fisher, 2001).
- To get a wider perspective on the credibility of authorities, consider reading accounts of how science has made its share of mistakes. (Youngson, 1998).

IRRELEVANT FALLACIES

We now turn to a different group of fallacies that are close cousins to the authority ones just discussed. Both kinds will distract you away from main issues by calling your attention away from central issues to side issues. In terms of authority, the distraction is to the power of the authority. In terms of *irrelevant fallacies,* the distractions include trying to discredit the person (or source) who presents the argument at hand rather than addressing the argument itself, or a ploy by which you are forced or made to feel pity in order to accept an argument, or an appeal is made to ignorance, or an attack is made on a made up argument or point. These are all irrelevant fallacies, and we will examine them in turn.

The Red Herring

The quintessential means to draw attention away from the issue at hand is the *red herring*. This is also known by other names such as ignoring the issue, befogging the issue, and diversion. It has no particular form or direction. It simply uses any means necessary to draw attention away from the main point of an argument. Incidentally, it gets its name from how prison escapees would drag dried herring across their trail in order to throw off tracking dogs (Engel, 1976).

Some individuals are adept at using this fallacy when they want to steer the direction of an argument, particularly if under attack. They distract you from the subject at hand and onto something else. For example: Critic: "Will the administrator of the Sunshine Treatment Center please tell me why he has done nothing to improve the relapse rate from his program?" Sunshine Administrator: "I resent that accusation. My program has been instrumental in bringing more jobs to this community and eliminating some of the unemployment that has plagued this region."

Attack the Person

Some authors, workshop leaders, or supervisors who run into counterarguments or are confronted with the lack of evidence in their claims often try to rebound from their obvious embarrassment and criticize the person who has created the counterargument. This fallacy is called *ad hominem*. The attack can be simple, like "Who do you think you are?" Or it can be more complex: "I suppose you hold some kind of advanced degree in research." These and similar statements are meant to make the one who leveled the counterargument look bad. The point here is that if you cannot win an argument on its merits then try to discredit the one who is coming after you. Question the person so that you damage his or her reputation. Once the reputation is damaged, what trusted information could possibly come from such a source? The ad hominem fallacy has nothing to do with the point of the argument. Its job is to draw you away from the real argument or issue.

There are a number of ways to conduct a personal attack. First, you can demean a person's character. For example, point out that your opponent has a dangerous anger streak, or lacks self-control. This particular attack's aim is to convince you that people with such character flaws are not to be trusted. Distrust in the person equals distrust in that person's argument. Second, assault the person's associates, background, or habits. For instance, people who affiliate with certain political parties or religious groups are easy targets for the ad hominem. Demean the associates, (e.g., How can you trust a Democrat or a Baptist?). The same applies to background (culture, historical period, education, etc.) or habits (e.g., this person is known to be forgetful). One sometimes sees this fallacy directed at a staff member who criticizes an administrator. The administrator may try to discredit the staff member with the goal of persuading other staff members to believe the discrediting statements and distance themselves from the critical one.

Use any of these tactics and you have committed the ad hominem fallacy.

There is a strong attraction to this particular fallacy because most of us get some level of satisfaction from seeing certain individuals humiliated or discredited. We have to be doubly on guard not to resort to this fallacy ourselves.

Questionable Sources

A spin on the ad hominem is the *damn the origin fallacy.* In this case, you don't attack a person, you attack the source of information. For instance, many addiction theories are written in journals, magazines, or aired in workshops. If I want to demean a particular theory I don't like, I can attack the source (not the argument) by stating, "Oh, that's a crappy magazine, and anything that comes out of it isn't worth much." This can achieve the same result as attacking the person. Attack the source, which implies if the source is bad the argument has also got to be bad.

The general critical thinking response to the use of this fallacy is to ask the attacker to respond to the argument and not to the source.

Two Wrongs Fallacy

Another spin on the ad hominem is to point out that the person does not practice what he/she preaches. This is called the *two wrongs fallacy* (Hughes, 2000). Adolescents often resort to this fallacy when parents begin to talk to them about drugs. A typical retort to a parent who is giving advice against drug use is "Well, you did it when you were my age." This statement has a lot of psychological power. However, just because a parent did illegal drugs does not make it right for the adolescent to do the same thing. Two wrongs do not make a right.

Appeal to Force

The next fallacy that draws your attention away from central issues is an *appeal to force.* Here, you are exposed to excessive economic, physical, or other forms of pressure in order to be made to fall in line with a certain way of thinking. For example, a supervisor can coerce a counselor to adopt a particular philosophy of treatment if a promotion or pay raise is on the line. One can also be threatened with a lawsuit as a show of force. However, the classical show of force is when two people get into a really nasty disagreement and one says to the other, "Let's go outside and settle this." This stupid remark is supposed to have us believe that whoever wins the physical fight also wins the argument.

An appeal to force directly related to the addiction field occurs when a counselor says to a client, "You do recovery my way or it's the highway." If the therapy doesn't proceed in a certain prescribed way, and if that way doesn't suit the client, the client can leave therapy. Then the client would have to face the consequences of an angry parole officer, spouse, or employer. This is a real show of force. Forcing someone to adapt to a certain therapy is simply not ethical and should not be tolerated in any field.

Appeal to Pity

Close to the appeal to force is the *appeal to pity.* At the core of this fallacy is the notion that you should feel sorry for me so I can have my way. Force is still being used but it's emotional. For example, medical personnel working for hospital detoxification units or inpatient programs often hear clients beg for medications to alleviate withdrawal symptoms long after the withdrawal has ended, or repeatedly ask for mood-altering meds for some unsubstantiated pain. It is difficult to turn down a tearful client with a "feel sorry for me" voice. So, sometimes mood-altering prescriptions are given when they are not needed.

On the other hand, one should not fall into the trap of believing that all such requests are bogus and should be regarded as a ploy to get drugs. That stance is uncaring and even unethical. An in-depth and proper assessment can usually distinguish between an appeal that is honest and one that is not.

Appeal to Ignorance

Another fallacy in this general group is the *appeal to ignorance (Ad Ignorantium).* This fallacy assumes that in some mysterious way the absence of evidence supports something as true. That's right. Some people would have you believe that just because something cannot be proved otherwise, it therefore must be true. The classic forms of this fallacy are found in the tabloid newspapers that line the checkout counters at your local supermarket. Many gullible people believe tales of bizarre creatures and strange night sightings because there isn't any proof against them (e.g., Bigfoot, UFOs).

More to our point are the suggestions some addiction counselors make in terms of clinical strategies. They often follow a pattern like this one: "Since no one can think of an alternative to the idea I have, it has to be a good one." Over the years I have heard a number of addiction counselors tell clients that a certain form of addiction counseling works because no one has ever found evidence that says it doesn't, so do what you're told. Some variations to the ignorance argument include the belief that all opinions should be considered no matter what they are. For example, there's the claim, "That's my opinion, and no matter what you say I'm not going to change it." I have actually heard people say, "I never saw any clients suffer if they stopped all their prescribed medications, so let's get them off all those drugs." This sentiment implies that because I haven't seen such a thing then it cannot exist. People who accept conclusions such as this are exhibiting major uncritical thinking (Tavris & Wade, 1995). Medications are prescribed by a trained physician who knows a lot more about prescription medications than laypeople.

Sometimes, the appeal to ignorance comes across in the claim that one cannot explain the success of one's program—it just works. What they cannot explain remains enigmatic, somehow mysterious, and meant to show that the program works. This bizarre conclusion is often delivered in a very confident tone; the inscrutability of the program is what makes it true! Once you buy the idea that a program is inscrutable and thus beyond explanation, you can be sold the Brooklyn Bridge. Science does not work this way (see Chapter 6). The response to the person who tries to get away with an appeal to ignorance is to ask for data and evidence.

Straw Man

This is one of those fallacies that you often, and sadly, see in our literature. It tries to falsify a position taken by another person and then pounce on that false position. It is much easier to attack the false image you just created than it is to attack the real issue. Create a phony image of something or someone, attack that phony image, and you have created a *straw man.*

Some people will try to tell you what another person is thinking or what that person really means. Now the speaker may not really know exactly what is on the mind of the other person, but will give you an interpretation, the fallacy user's interpretation. That's the straw man, which is more easily attacked.

The straw man is especially prevalent in politics. For example, when one candidate begins to tell you what his/her opponent's views are you can bet a straw man is about to appear. Such attacks are rarely based on fact but mostly on misrepresentations. The same applies to angry authors or administrators who, in order to defend themselves, tell you what their opponent is thinking. First they present you with the straw man, and then attack what they just made up.

You can counter this fallacy by asking, if not demanding, what the real position to be addressed is. Accuracy is the key to demolishing a straw man.

CHAPTER SUMMARY

Authority Fallacies

- We buy into authorities and their fallacies because we have been taught to respect them and they come across in a very convincing manner.
- Addiction counselors fall into the authority trap because they believe people more than they believe research.
- True authorities back up their claims with credible research.
- Folk wisdom is often the basis of doctrines and memes.
- Do what everyone else is doing and you appeal to the fallacy of the many.
- Although they can be emotionally moving, testimonials and anecdotes are not science.
- The most effective strategy you can use to avoid these mind traps is to question and have a good knowledge of the latest research.

Irrelevant Fallacies

- Irrelevant fallacies draw your attention away from the point of an argument. There are a number of ways to do that.
- One way is to use the ad hominem fallacy. Attack the person, discredit him/her, and that is supposed to discredit the argumentor the source.
- The two wrongs fallacy: (because you did it, so can I). But two wrongs don't make it right.
- The appeal to force: (It's my way or the highway).
- The appeal to pity ("I need morphine or I will die").
- The appeal to ignorance (I can't disprove it, so it has to be true).
- The straw man fallacy: falsifying the facts and attacking the bogus image just created.

CHAPTER NINE

Causal Fallacies and Weak Inductions

This chapter discusses causal and weak induction fallacies. *Causal fallacies* make errors in cause-and-effect reasoning. *Weak induction fallacies* make errors by not supplying enough evidence to support a conclusion. We first review causal fallacies.

CAUSAL ARGUMENTS

Before we examine these fallacies we need to get a clear idea of what exactly a causal or connecting argument is. A causal argument says that one thing causes another (X causes Y) (Levy, 1997; Moore & Parker, 1995). (You might want to go back to Chapter 5 and look at the diagrams to refresh your memory.)

The addiction field is filled with clinically researched causal examples. For example:

- Heavy and prolonged drinking can cause certain cancers.
- Heavy and prolonged drinking causes liver damage.
- Heavy and prolonged drinking causes Korsakoff's syndrome.
- Heavy and prolonged drug and/or alcohol use causes changes in brain neurotransmitters.
- Smoking causes lung cancer.

The truth of these causal statements is obvious to any well-informed addiction professional. Yet, counselors and other professionals sometimes try to infer that one thing caused another using weak arguments, which can lead to clinical and other problems. We outline a few to beware of.

X caused Y—When in Fact It Didn't

A causal fallacy seen all too often in the addiction field is *making the wrong connection,* and can best be illustrated by an example.

Treatment programs tend to attribute their effectiveness to certain underlying philosophies and methods. This is called an illusory connection. Why illusory? Because client improvement is erroneously connected to certain treatment strategies or program styles. The problem with such claims is that they never convincingly demonstrate that there is a direct connection between a particular intervention and recovery. No research has ever credibly indicated that intervention "x" caused outcome "y." Even with the finest research designs and statistical methods, the best we seem to be able to do is to demonstrate certain *correlations* between a treatment and its outcome. That is, there is some relationship between "x" and "y", but it is not causal.

Why this lack of cause and effect? Well, we can't say with any certainty that one specific thing actually causes another in terms of addiction treatment. There are too many other variables that influence outcome. In order to say there is a direct connection, one would have to control for all the social, psychological, and even biological influences that could have had as much to do with someone getting sober as the treatment program. Yes, there is good evidence that therapy works as opposed to no therapy. But trying to find out what it is within therapy that makes the difference is difficult.

Of the current counseling treatments available, none has been shown to be more effective than any other (Institute of Medicine, 1990). That conclusion was written more than a decade ago and is still valid today. Formal treatments work only marginally better than the natural (untreated) state of recovery (Seligman, 1993). Yet, many programs go to great pains to promote analysis, cognitive therapy, cognitive-behavioral therapy, community therapy, or whatever, as the most successful interventions available. One constantly hears, "How can you argue with success?" Well, this very perception is deficient (Dawes, 1994). Some people will get over a problem without treatment. Yet, a treatment program whose clients have improved and at the same time were attending AA, NA, MM, SOS, starting a new job, and had a good support system post treatment will attribute any success to itself.

People in the field seem to have a halo effect to their favorite treatment. As noted, if presented with contrary evidence most people will find new ways to justify and confirm why they think what a correlation should be (Piattelli-Palmarini, 1994).

There is no way to evaluate such conclusions because we cannot compare what did happen to what might have happened had AA, NA, MM, or a selected therapy been unavailable. The fallacy here is that we think the influence of an intervention would have occurred if we had not done what we did. This is called a *hypothetical counterfactual.* It is hypothetical because we can never be certain of "what would have happened if" (Dawes, 1994).

The problem with trying to determine what causes what is that it can lead to wrong connections. Clinicians will often have expectations and use fallacies that distort their interpretations of observations. As this book has been trying to point out, fallacies are everywhere and influence everything. Remember that the dynamics of addiction are complex, and require complex answers.

Recommendations to use in the ongoing battle to thwart wrong connections include the following:

1. Remember that there has never been any definitive evidence that one form of counseling strategy causes recovery. Rather, recovery rests on a combination of things.
2. Pay attention to cases that do not confirm your favored ideas.
3. Be cautious about believing that one form of treatment causes recovery because you expect it to.
4. Be doubly cautious of people in the addiction field who claim to have found the secret of successful treatment. If such claims were true we would have had addiction cured by now.

That Has to Be the Real Cause (Maybe Not)

The next causal irrationality is *misplaced causality* (Piattelli-Palmarini, 1994). In this case, the fallacy assigns a cause to an array of causes that are available from a number of possible, if not equally relevant, causes. For example, the suggested causes for addiction are often stated in such terms as some spiritual/existential state of destitution, repressed anger and rage, or the cunning and baffling nature of the substance itself. Some of these theories have a sensible ring to them and some do not. A sensible theory might be that certain biological determinants contribute to an addiction. Another theory attributes addiction to an oral fixation, which doesn't sound so sensible.

At this stage of addiction research, we cannot predict who will become alcoholic or drug addicted (Seligman, 1993). Yet, many in the field will get caught up in an error of causal reasoning, believing if event "x" happens, it leads to behavior "y." If it were not for this error of thinking many an addiction self-help book would not have been written and accepted in the past fifty years.

A corollary to this conspicuous fallacy is attributing an effect to an insignificant cause. Some counselors push their own agenda and believe that "x" really is causing "y," when in reality that belief (e.g., unresolved anger) has less of an effect on the situation than other, more substantive causes (e.g., biology).

Suggestions for how to offset this and the remaining fallacies are found at the end of this chapter.

What Came First

This next causal fallacy is called *post hoc, ergo propter hoc,* meaning after this, therefore because of this, sometimes called the *false cause.* Many people believe that just because something occurred before an event, that something must be its cause. For example, say the refrigerator in your new apartment stopped working the day you moved in. If it did, then you must be the cause of the malfunctioning refrigerator. Silly isn't it, but some people would believe you really were the cause.

Confidence solely in this cause-to-effect route is bound to have therapeutic implications. For example, there was a time when it was believed that a person's problems were the cause of alcohol and drug use. The problems came first and obviously had to be the cause of an increase in drinking and drug use. Many a therapist would work hard to resolve those problems, believing the abusive drinking would stop if the problem was solved. The difficulty with this approach was that no attempt was made to address the drinking, and the client would continue to drink even though some resolution of the problem took place.

At the same time, many hold that it is the drinking and drugs that cause a person's problems. Here the therapeutic effort is aimed at stopping the drinking, in the belief that this will make things better. Although this is often true, there are cases where it is not. These simple after-the-fact counseling methods have been replaced with more complex treatments that address the whole person and do not rely on such simplistic reasoning.

An additional muddying issue in this "causing this or that" talk is the issue of events that are bi-directional. What if one event does not follow another, but both events cause one another (Levy, 1997)?

An illustration of this fallacy is the issue of disease. Traditionally, we have assumed that a true disease needed a physical cause like a germ or genetic anomaly. This type of thinking has been the Achilles heel of the disease model of addiction because no such causes have been found. Many heated exchanges have taken place over this issue (Peele, 1988; Wallace, 1989). Yet, this whole causal factor argument may be irrelevant in that those who have addiction problems have them because of the direct intake of psychoactive chemicals. It is the abuse of drugs and alcohol that results in the disease (Wallace, 1996). This line of argument may be all the more irrelevant in that researchers have not found a common cause for both.

It Stands Out, So It Has To Be the Cause

Another causal thinking error occurs because we are strongly influenced by the nature of effects. In other words, the more striking or dramatic the forerunning event, the more likely we are to perceive it as the main cause. For example, clients who have a long personal alcoholic history are often thought to have come from an alcoholic family (genetic factor), inappropriate modeling, and some level of abuse. All are striking variables that can be easily related to addiction almost without thought. And yes, some of these variables do indeed correlate highly with addiction, but this is not always true. Yet, many addiction practitioners will insist that long-term drinking cases must have a familial cause. Such thinking can lead to a misapplication of treatment interventions to a client who does not neatly fall into any of the striking variables listed above.

Addiction administrators are not immune to the striking fallacy. Some have been known to attribute the cause of dwindling program loyalty to striking presumptions of ingratitude, betrayal, or fickleness.

The striking fallacy can also be observed on a larger scale. For example, many addiction authors and workshop providers cite a striking personality feature as the cause of an addiction. Sometimes that assumption is accurate, sometimes not. For example, many people will be honest in one situation and without blinking an eye lie in another. A small lie to the boss is told without much concern, whereas dishonesty to one's spouse would not be tolerated. In such situations, what then are the striking personality traits that cross all states of affairs? Traits vary according to the situation. If I happen to see the liar in action I could mistakenly say that lying is a striking personality trait. If I see the truth-teller in another situation, I could mistakenly label honesty as the most striking trait. And if I do that in social situations, I am likely to do the same thing in clinical situations, which may skew treatment planning.

This striking fallacy brings up the issue of the *fundamental attribution error,* which is a tendency to ascribe the actions of people to their personality traits, but not to a situation (Levy, 1997). We all have the tendency to judge the actions of others in terms of their traits and characteristics, rather than the circumstances of a situation. Thinking this way automatically sets us up to judge people rather than their actions. With the attribution error, find the cause in the individual.

For the addiction professional this can have devastating effects. We can wrongly attribute a problem to some imbedded personality trait and not the situation in which it was revealed. One illustration of this attribution error is to claim that a client is not being honest in a group when in fact the client is shy in groups. The same holds for an intake situation, where we might think the client is guarded and elusive when this behavior is a variable of the circumstance: the client doesn't like sharing personal history with strangers. Yet, once such a judgment is made it is difficult to change.

I Had It, They Have It, So That's the Cause

The last causal thinking errors examined in this set have to do with personal interactions. Those who have had personal experiences with an addiction tend to believe that their addiction was caused by the same thing that caused another's addiction. They are trying to tie a causal link between act and outcome. That is the cause of one addiction may be similar to the cause of another, but they are by no means the same. To base clinical decisions on this fallacy is an injustice to the client. Addiction has multiple causes. Base clinical decisions on the causal factors for the client, not what caused your own addiction.

To address this set of causal fallacies, the following are recommended:

1. Just because a reported cause of addiction is striking, available, and sounds reasonable is no guarantee that it had anything to do with true causes.
2. Suspect any explanation if there is little if any research to back up its claim.
3. Consider whether an event can have alternative causes and explanations.
4. Cause and effect do not always follow one another. Sometimes effect precedes an assumed cause, or both can seem to cause each other.
5. Be skeptical of causal relationships where a great deal of emotion is associated with a purported cause. Good causes have solid theories behind them.
6. Just because I have a problem and my client has a similar one, there is a high probability that they will not have the same set of causes.

It Happened; Now I Can Explain It

After-the-fact reasoning is the last causal fallacy to be addressed here. We are all prone to armchair philosophy. That is, we tend to try to make sense of things after they happen. Following some major world event, you can hear people everywhere say, "I knew that was going to happen." Many of us will go into detail explaining our reasons for a family, social, national, or international incident.

It makes us sound smart and gives a wonderful boost to our egos. However, no foreknowledge was ever mentioned prior to the incident to account for the presumed accuracy of our after-the-fact reasoning.

Let's take an example of after-the-fact reasoning from the addiction field. Suppose a client leaves a program and is reported to have relapsed shortly following discharge. You can be sure that in a staff meeting that client will be the talk of the table. Everyone will be armchair theorizing as to why the client relapsed. Conjectures and rationalizations will fly and in some cases even a consensus will be reached. The staff will correlate all kinds of unsubstantiated ideas with the relapse, saying the client should have been confronted more, or stayed in the program longer, or seen more educational films. It sounds good, but the fact remains that this type of theorizing is done after the fact. At this point, anyone can sound right. This rationalizing helps many a counselor go home with a clear conscience.

To offset the after-the-fact fallacy is simple. Make your theories known *before* a discharge or other similar event. Then compare your results and brace yourself for a helping of humble pie.

FALLACIES OF WEAK INDUCTION

Recall that induction is the process of gathering facts to build a significant or reasonable case that a conclusion is accurate. There are, however, a host of fallacies that argue a point without resorting to evidence or facts. These fallacies depend on weak support between premises and conclusions. They supply a small amount of evidence to support a conclusion, so at best, the evidence is limited (Hurley, 1997). Anyone can argue for a conclusion based on insufficient or distorted facts. We all do it. Believing limited evidence can trap the unsuspecting.

Don't Have Enough Facts? Make Assumptions Anyway

The *hasty generalization* (overgeneralizing) is probably the most blatant example of drawing meaning from little or no evidence. In fact, that's all it is—deriving or jumping to a conclusion before sufficient evidence or enough facts are gathered. Sufficient evidence generally means you have a large enough sample from which to draw a reliable conclusion. But some people jump to a conclusion based on a small sample size or one that is atypical of the population under investigation. Small or atypical samples do not represent a true population.

The seduction of this common fallacy is that a small sample appears to provide a reasonable explanation of things. However, such seemingly reasonable explanations are often wrong and tend to stereotype. There are a number of levels where this occurs. We will look at two: the clinical and program levels.

Hasty Generalizations at the Clinical Level

An illustration of the hasty generalization fallacy at the clinical level occurred some time ago when I worked in a rehabilitation center treating adolescents with addiction problems. I noted that soon after counselors would take over a caseload of adolescents, the conversation around the lunch table turned to generalizing. A counselor would make a statement that our clients symbolize the way all adolescents behave. Other counselors would chime in with a similar sentiment, and thereafter all adolescents everywhere were labeled addicted or soon to become addicted. Daily exposure to the same atypical example might lead even the best counselor to believe that the country's youth are headed to hell in a hand-basket. But that's the problem: the small sample is not indicative of the larger adolescent group. Over 20 years later, predictions about great proportions of youth in America becoming addicted has proved wrong.

The main problem with drawing conclusions based on small, if not atypical samples, is that it gives rise to prejudices, which create problems with clinical decision perceptions. In the case just cited, the hasty generalization fallacy clouded the thinking of those counselors and contributed to negative views of all teenagers. In those days, our relapse rate was admittedly high, and yet new clients were generalized as losers with little hope of recovery from the day of their admission. Now, that's a lousy way for any professional to view a new client!

If this group of counselors had taken the time to get more information about the big picture of adolescents, things would have been different at the facility. Large samples provide a much more accurate base and tell a more accurate story about a population.

Hasty Generalizations at the Program Level

Another example of generalizing occurs at the program level. Small samples are used to tell prospective clients and referral sources how effective certain programs are. The samples used are not always representative of the total population, but they are dramatic and available. Now if we believe in the reliability of the small sample, we can embrace certain ideas. For example, many treatment outcome studies have indicated that by attending a certain program an addicted person's chances of recovery are greater than ninety percent. On closer examination, many of these facilities did not include all the samples they should have. They reported only those clients who were successful completers and did not include those who dropped out of treatment or other such negative influence samples. This casts suspicion on the population in question. One has to be suspicious when programs report such high success rates based on skewed samples.

Small samples can lead to reporting false positives and false negatives. We discussed this before but it needs to be stated again for the hasty generalization fallacy. A false positive indicates that something is true when it is really false, and a false negative indicates that something is false when it is really true. The formulas many of you were exposed to in your first and second statistical classes are designed to avoid these contingencies. And yes, statistics can be manipulated. Not using the correct formula for a certain data set can lead to problems. One can obtain data that look good in one formula and not so good in another. This is a deliberate manipulation of sample data.

To guard against any hasty generalizations in addiction counseling is simple. Make sure that any conclusion is based on a sufficiently large sample. In addition, if a workshop presenter or professor makes what appears to be a generalization, ask to see the data. You have a right if not an obligation to do that. Developing a thorough understanding of statistics allows you more easily to spot the tendency to manipulate data.

More Generalizing

The fallacy to generalize too quickly doesn't stop with the hasty form. There is one other generalizing fallacy often seen in the addiction field that needs attention.

If generalizing too quickly doesn't represent a population under scrutiny, there is one form of this fallacy that deliberately does. It is *exclusive generalizing*. Talk to anyone who is truly knowledgeable in the field about what causes an addiction and you will get a complex answer because addiction is a complex disorder. However, some authors have written books and articles that tell us that the onset of addiction can be reduced to a simple or singular explanation, which does not account for other possibilities. For example, it has been purported that the onset of addiction is due to spiritual deprivation, anger, unresolved grief (unresolved anything), a deprived childhood, repressed memories, bad genes, resentment, or any of the seven deadly sins, among other things. If you can name a negative human emotion or condition, someone somewhere has probably written an article saying that it is the core issue that leads to an addiction. This inclusiveness fallacy has also been applied to relapse dynamics, basic recovery conditions, and family interactions.

Although all these theories sound good in a lecture or on paper, they don't consider other complex factors that contribute to this problem. If a clinician buys into a simple explanation, that clinician's assessment and subsequent treatment are going to be myopic, and stand a good chance of missing the mark.

The recommended antidote to simplifying addiction or any human condition to a single cause is to use one's critical thinking skills. If addiction was as simple as some experts have claimed it to be, we would have found concrete and verifiable solutions to this problem a long time ago. If I can be exclusive, I can also be *inclusive*. This means I can include all kinds of reasons for an addiction. The problem with inclusiveness (as we saw in Chapter 5) is that it waters down the parameters of addiction and ends up saying nothing. A few addiction-oriented books written back in the 1980s were guilty of this dilution, citing everything but the kitchen sink as a cause of addiction.

In line with these particular fallacies is the issue of *representativeness* (Shermer, 1997). This fallacy uses our propensity to remember our successes rather than our failures. Certain programs have this tendency. A prospective customer or referral source can buy into these selected successes and not think about questioning any failures. If taken in by the representativeness fallacy, we have fallen prey to a selected if not biased sample. Be suspicious of programs and counselors who claim high rates of success without doing a research analysis of that success.

These generalizing fallacies set the stage for the next three fallacies.

Talk About Weak Support

A blatant form of providing feeble support for a conclusion, these fallacies are called *ignoring the evidence, unrepresentative thinking,* or *confirmation bias* (Shermer, 2001). When people resort to these fallacies, they simply neglect information that doesn't agree with a favored theory or idea. The omitted evidence could be a confounding variable that casts some shadow on or is the polar opposite of a favored theory (Piattelli-Palmarini, 1994).

As noted in previous chapters, those of us with a strong opinion about something are often loath to change it. We remain steadfast even if the evidence and data are overwhelmingly against us. Moreover, most of us do not like to admit we are wrong. For some addiction professionals, admitting to a wrong belief is equated with diminished self-esteem and prestige. They trust their clichés over any additional information brought to bear on an issue and will engage in arguments that include out-and-out discard for valuable research evidence.

For another example of this fallacy, check the reference section books and note that when some authors wish to present a certain theory their references will be the ones that support the theme of the book and nothing else.

In my travels, I have presented reliable research information on certain addiction subjects only to have it brushed aside in favor of the unrepresentative and flimsy data used to support a favored point of view. For example, not too long ago I attempted to present data that indicated that no one treatment method has been shown to be more effective than another, only to have the data completely ignored and usurped by personal testimony.

People have a tendency to process only that information that adds to their belief system. We tend to accept information we understand unless there are clear and compelling reasons not to (Carlson, 1995). People in the addiction field who pledge allegiance to a certain idea or theory often associate only with those who support the same views, or subscribe only to reading material that is in line with their preferred views. This myopic perspective does not lead to critical thinking.

It is rare to find someone who advocates that addiction is a disease, habit, or moral model turn around in the same article or book and promote data of an opposing idea. Now that is critical thinking.

To offset this powerful fallacy strive to:

1. Look for evidence that argues against your cherished beliefs. Don't discount that information, but use it to expand the horizons of your thought.
2. Try to tolerate and accept ideas and evidence that are adversarial. This process will challenge you and may give you new ideas.
3. If an idea conflicts with your beliefs, hold it in your mind rather than immediately tossing it away. Now, try to account for the conflict in some rational manner. If you don't have a workable plan to answer that question, develop one.
4. In the addiction field, no one is always right!

Just Don't Understand

This next irrationality is *misinterpreting of evidence.* Here evidence is misjudged, not understood, or misread. To illustrate, most addiction professionals' knowledge of statistics is rudimentary at best. Ask a sample of them to distinguish a t-test from an ANOVA, and most will not know what you are talking about. As a result, data that come from that realm are often viewed with suspicion. Recall that statistics is not in the same domain as typical day-to-day clinical thinking. The latter is based on building clinical conclusions from various data. Research and statistics are more in the "what's the sample or population about" realm, and how to make sure that a hypothesis will achieve significance. Evidence from one domain does not translate well to the other. Hence, a little suspicion as to what camp is more relevant or accurate exists and the data can easily be misinterpreted.

When clinicians confront statistical data, misunderstanding and suspicion often set in "Anybody can manipulate statistics" may be the rallying cry. To a point this is true, but if statistical data are cited in a journal report you can bet that those statistics have been scrutinized by an editorial board to make sure no manipulation took place. If any irregularities are found, you can also bet that a loud cry of "error" and "lack of significance" will be heard. The same cannot be said for intuition, which is often the end product of irrational deliberation. Yet, many addiction professionals demean statistics and laud hunches.

To address the fallacy of misinterpreting evidence:

1. Take a research and statistics course.
2. Balance the intuitive nature of counseling with the scientific.
3. Ask somebody to help you understand data if you cannot. A little humility goes a long way.

Can't Live With Conflicting Information? Alter It

The next irrationality focuses not on ignoring evidence but on *distorting* it. Sometimes we will twist what we hear or read to fit our notion of things. For example, upon reading a national statistic on the spread of a new illicit drug, some individuals will distort it to make the data sound either much worse or much better than the original statistic intended. If I look on the darker side of life, then my read on the spread of a new street drug will distort in the dark direction. If I look on the brighter side of things, I may well underestimate the spread of the new street drug. If I'm an administrator reviewing next year's budget, I can distort figures to reflect the inability to come up with promised pay raises. Or I can begin work on a long-term improvement project that cannot be completed because I read too much into the same budget figures.

Once a distorted explanation takes hold it is difficult to change. For example, in completing a clinical assessment on a new client, if a counselor wedded to a certain theory (e.g., disease model, analytical, or motivational theory) uncovers something that does not fit that theory, then some level of dissonance is going to arise. In this discordant state, something has to give, and sometimes it is the facts of the case. That is, the facts are sometimes stretched to fit a prevailing personal or program theory. If a counselor is heavily invested in some addiction model and the model is faced with conflicting data, then one way to solve the problem is to alter the facts to fit the theory. Needless to say, this kind of thinking can have a devastating effect on evaluations and diagnoses.

Altering of the facts has been observed in many a staff meeting. If a counselor is invested, let's say, in the "inner child" dynamic, and information is given that contradicts that framework, you may hear the invested counselor say something like, "Well, of course, this is an inner child issue. Can't you see that inner child dynamics account for those facts too?" This is the bending of the behavior to fit the theory, and it creates a serious problem. Neither the client nor the information is seen accurately. Such fact altering is a great detriment to quality treatment, and an ethical issue as well.

As noted, the tenacity with which people will hold on to obviously flawed ideas is remarkable. Generally, once we draw a conclusion, we pull in anything we can to support that conclusion. If there are opposing perspectives, most people will first attempt to contort or reject the opposition in order to keep the original conclusion inviolate.

Recommendations to combat this irrationality include:

1. Rather than distort opposing evidence, especially in the case of a client, consider it carefully. Could such information be of assistance in a treatment direction and contribute to a quality recovery process? Critical thinkers don't distort facts. They adjust their ideas to fit the facts not adjust the facts to fit the theory.
2. As we have noted, be cautious about your memory. Remember that you are most likely to recall whatever fits into your prevailing notions.
3. Also remember that changing one's mind is a sign of strength, not weakness.
4. Be doubly aware of the explanations that you use to champion your pet views.

CHAPTER SUMMARY

Causal Fallacies

- Saying that one thing causes another is subject to a number of fallacies.
- If you claim that one thing causes another when it doesn't, you've made the wrong connection fallacy.

- You can mistake a cause by thinking it is a prominent one and therefore has to be *the* cause.
- Just because one thing follows another does not make it a cause-and-effect situation. Believe that it is and you have committed the fallacy of "after this, therefore because of this." What if both events are causing each other?
- Despite the allure of the "more striking/dramatic the event the more likely it is the cause of something," it could just as well not be so.
- Believing that because I've had the same problem you have makes me an expert on you is a fallacy of personal interaction.
- Try theorizing *before* something happens and check closely to see if it did. If you are accurate and can maintain this accuracy, call me. I want to talk to you; otherwise be careful of the "after the fact" theories.

Weak Induction Fallacies

Weak support between premises and conclusions is the theme for this set of fallacies. They come in several forms.

- Hastily generalize before you have a good set of facts.
- Reduce complex conditions to a simple set of ideas and commit an exclusive generalizing fallacy.
- Include all sorts of reasons for the onset of an addiction (or the reasons for anything) and you commit an inclusive generalizing fallacy
- To commit an unrepresentative thinking fallacy, don't accept what the facts tell you. Ignore them, and look only for evidence that supports your conclusions.
- Misinterpret evidence and don't make an effort to really understand it.
- If you can't live with the facts, distort them.

CHAPTER TEN

Fallacies That Presume a Conclusion Before It Is Proven and Classification Fallacies

This chapter looks at two sets of fallacies. The first set of broad fallacies deceives by making you believe that they address the facts of an argument, but in reality they don't. They provide the answers they want to their own questions. A fancy way of saying the same is that such fallacies suppose an illegitimate assumption (Conway & Munson, 1997). The second set of fallacies concerns ambiguity and related problems that affect a classification. We begin with the presuming and deceiving types of fallacies.

PRESUMPTION FALLACIES

Begging the Question

The first example is a classic case of presumption. It settles a question by simply reasserting a position. Remember in Chapter 5 we laid out how an argument is supposed to work. It should have premises that support a conclusion. *Begging the question* declares a certainty in its very premises. The premises turn out to be the conclusion. This fallacy merely repeats what it claims to be true. For example, someone who states, "I believe the disease concept (place your own favorite model here) of alcoholism is the best explanation of alcoholism dynamics because it is superior to all others" has just begged the question. The claim has not come from a true argument, but from the premises just stated. Similar examples include the "fact" that alcoholism has to be a habit, moral failing, and so forth, because "that is what it really is," and that's the way I want the answer to the question of "what is addiction?" to turn out. These fallacies are redundant, circular, and really say nothing.

Gambrill (1990) notes several variations to begging the question. One involves claiming something is obvious and certain without any evidence (e.g., "It is a well accepted fact that 'X' brand of therapy works best"). Another uses emotionally loaded words to influence an unsuspecting recipient (e.g., "I feel with all my heart and soul," or "the moral model of addiction towers above all others in accuracy and truth"). Another uses the ploy of altering a definition rather than admit to a counterexample. The classic illustration is that alcoholics who return to social drinking were never alcoholics to begin with.

To engage this fallacy critically, point out the circular argument and ask the person who made it to present data to support his/her conclusion.

False Dichotomy

Either the client in question is an alcoholic or not. Have you ever heard that statement? If you have and you responded with one of the two options, then you fell for the *false dichotomy, either-or* fallacy.

This fallacy presumes that there are only two possibilities for a certain condition when in fact there may be many. Getting used to the idea of many possibilities for a certain conclusion or outcome is a difficult one to shed because humans naturally seem to think only in dichotomies not in many possibilities (Kerlinger, 1986). So, the false dichotomy is a potent fallacy. Those who use it often secretly prefer one alternative and delude you into agreeing with their position. If you don't agree, you can usually expect to be attacked by another set of fallacies.

The problem with the either/or fallacy is that the options are insufficient. To assume that the complex problem of addiction can be reduced to just two possibilities is just plain wrong.

You can also see this fallacy being used by some so-called addiction experts. When they write or make a presentation, they dichotomize their arguments. The claim they don't want you to accept is discredited, while the other is given praise. The praised idea, of course, is the one the user of the ploy wants you to accept. Just remember that nothing in addiction studies is simple, and any theory needs evidence. Demeaning an oppositional stance while praising one's own solves nothing.

A good way out of this fallacy is to counter the either-or predicament by envisioning other possibilities. In the field of addiction, there are many. The other way out of this fallacy is to hit it head on and call it for what it is—a fallacy.

The Slippery Slope

We all have heard predictions. They vary within the political, social, religious, and economic realms. A classic example was the domino theory that if one country fell to communism, another and then another would fall. These predictions are based on a presumed set of chain reactions, which, if set in motion, will supposedly result in some dire consequence for humanity. It is generally known as the *slippery slope* fallacy.

This fallacy has been used in the addiction field in a number of ways. One doomsday forecast made not too long ago was the demise of our field because of managed care. Another was that if college courses and workshops started teaching anything other than the disease model, there would be a significant increase in the number of people with addictions. Yet another was that the use of cocaine would become uncontrolled and raise the addiction level to epidemic proportions. You can bet that any time a new drug hits the populace someone somewhere is going to make a slippery slope argument.

Clients in treatment programs have been told that if they don't behave in a certain way they will certainly doom themselves. There is often a lot of emotional conviction attached to this slippery slope prediction, which makes it seem all the more credible. The retort to this fallacy is one we have mentioned several times already: Addiction and recovery are complex things that require complex predictions to arrive at a realistic and reasonable conclusion.

One last slippery slope example occurs in certain styles of prevention education. The more disaster-prone prevention education contains the "logical" statement that any form of drinking (especially by young people) will lead to more drinking and will eventually result in death. Aside from its inaccuracy, most students who hear this warning are not impressed and many scoff at the whole notion. Most people in the world drink and the drinking does not increase pathologically or end in premature death. In fact, some data indicate that a drink or two is good for you (Thun et al., 1997).

The way out of the slippery slope is similar to other suggestions we made. Ask to see the data.

CLASSIFICATION FALLACIES

Addiction counselors, prevention specialists, and supervisors look for and create classifications all the time. That's part of our job. We sort people into categories and diagnostic levels for example, gender, political affiliation, depressed, or alcohol dependent. Addiction studies workshops, college classes, and books present a number of classification systems. All clamor to be the system to use, and that's where problems arise. There is no one agreed-upon and definitive classification system in the addiction field. Even if there were, no two professionals are going to use a system the same way. Clients are going to be misclassified, and that creates serious problems.

Some counseling strategies that rely on a certain diagnosis do have a good treatment record. Knowing the most appropriate diagnosis will save time and effort by using a useful strategy (e.g., stress management techniques with certain anxiety disorders). Yet, all classification systems have limitations, even when used by trained professionals, and an addiction professional's personal construct system can sometimes add to errors. It is important to know some of those errors.

Everything Is the Same

Let's start with a particularly annoying classification fallacy called *stereotyping* (Gibbs & Gambrill, 1996). When I presume that certain attitudes or behaviors are applicable to an entire group, I have created a stereotype. A prejudice is the result of the stereotype, and that's the problem with creating stereotypes. A significant stereotype, and pardon me for repeating it, that most people with an alcohol addiction are con artists, manipulators, and in a high state of denial. These claims and similar ones create unwarranted stereotypes. No evidence to date has ever proved such a string of stereotypes for all people with an alcohol problem (Miller & Rollnick, 1991). Attitudes and behaviors for this population vary from to person to person. To believe otherwise is to distort your perception of a diverse and complex population. It is this distortion that leads to bad treatment interventions, negative program philosophies, and the writing of bad books. Stereotyping is a particularly pernicious fallacy in the addiction field. It only adds to the stigma of addiction.

In counseling, a fruitful alternative to the stereotype fallacy is to assess and judge clients individually. Period. Should you find yourself writing problem statements that all look alike you are probably drifting into stereotyping. Should you find that verbal reports to your supervisor and other staff have a similar ring, again you are drifting into stereotyping. You need to be very careful with this fallacy.

Imprecision

The use of *vague terms* is a serious fallacy closely related to stereotyping. You can clarify ambiguous terms because they are generally imprecise and can be made clear. But vague terms are vague by their very nature even if the context in which they are used is clear (Gambrill, 1990). Examples from the addiction field include such terms as resistance, adult children of alcoholics, or co-dependency. These and similar terms are so fuzzy that they can be applied to a number of different settings and people.

The simple solution to vague terms is to use more precise terms. Report the number of observed behaviors, or report behavior without vague commentary. If your language is less vague, it means your thinking is less vague as well. However, be careful not to overuse technical terms with clients, who may not understand what you mean.

Apples and Oranges

The last item in this section is the *incorrect classification* fallacy. We observe a set of behaviors and report the client as depressed when it is more likely to be a case of prolonged withdrawal from alcohol. Then we incorrectly classify because we rely on vague terms, which lead to ambiguous and often incorrect classifications.

An incorrect classification can also result from unreliable classification systems. Some classification devices used in the addiction field have virtually no parametric studies associated with them (e.g., Jellinek curve). If I have a head full of incorrect classifications, I am going to make many incorrect assumptions about things and people. Incorrect is incorrect. Using critical thinking, I can reduce the probability of this error.

CHAPTER SUMMARY

Presumption Fallacies

Want to win an argument? Presume you already have the answer by resorting to:

- Begging the question: make a claim and then declare that claim to be true.
- False dichotomy: claim only two possibilities when in reality many exist and add a convincing case for one of the possibilities.
- Slippery slope: predict catastrophe based on a simple presumption.

Classification Fallacies

- Misclassify and you create fallacies.
- Stereotyping is a major fallacy of classification in that it destroys an individual identity and creates a mass, usually inaccurate one.
- Vague terms and anything clinically imprecise are going to cause problems.
- Incorrect classifications are based on vague terms and poor assessment practices, which contribute to clinical mistakes.

CHAPTER ELEVEN

Fallacies Caused by Perception Problems and Fallacies of Manner and Style

For this last fallacy chapter, we take a look at fallacies that have more to do with our personal side: the way we perceive things around us and the problems our perceptions might cause, as well as our personal style that might get in the way of solid thinking.

FALLACIES RELATED TO PROBLEMS OF PERCEPTION

Perception is selective (Gambrill, 1990). No matter what our education or experience we constantly see ourselves, and others, through a perceptional lens called *assimilation bias* (Levy, 1997). That is, our brains are full of prejudices, propensities to categorize, unchallenged habits of thought, and automatic ordering of perception (Carter, 1998; Levy, 1997). These human tendencies either allow certain information to come unimpeded to our minds and change the way we think, or modify the new information to fit some internal schema we already have (Levy, 1997). These are the processes of *accommodation* or *assimilation*. They modify our thinking to fit reality or modify the facts to suit our perceptions. This section addresses some of these fallacies.

It Makes a Difference to Be First

Our first perceptional fallacy is called the *availability error* because we all have the tendency to judge something or someone by the first thing that comes to our mind (Garb & Boyle, 2003). For example, when you meet your next client, what was said in a recent training session comes to mind more easily than an older idea and you may find yourself categorizing a client in terms of the last workshop you attended. In addition, clinicians are more likely to diagnosis a particular problem if they have had recent experience with a similar case (Bensley, 1998). This is the power of availability.

Now we need to define "available" a little more precisely. Available material is the information that an addiction professional has most recently encountered or that produces strong emotion. It also includes the dramatic and concrete, and leaves the imprint of strong images in the mind.

Piattelli-Palmarini (1994) talks about this fallacy in terms of acquiescence or acceptance. That is, when faced with a reasonable method of solving a problem we usually accept it the way it was framed, and often don't look for alternative forms of resolution. This availability error gives rise to anchoring. That is, people, and most certainly addiction professionals, often remain anchored to their original opinion. We create first impressions that are difficult to change. Counselors who return from certain popular workshops often expound the new information they have just learned to all who will listen, and especially to their clients. They have acquiesced to a preferred mode or made a quick impression, (Piattelli-Palmarini, 1994). Sometimes, for years after being exposed to certain arguments, they will continue to interpret their clients and entire social systems in terms of how they acquired their original information. Often this is carried over into staff meetings, and whole programs can get caught up in the latest movement without any critical thinking taking place.

To offset this pernicious fallacy, always consider alternatives and question even your best formed conclusions.

The Preferred and the Not So Preferred

The very act of asking questions of a client can affect a perception. This phenomenon is called *reactivity* (Levy, 1997). Two associated biased outcomes are the thinking forms called the *halo* and the *devil effect.* Let's say you have a client in your caseload who has one strikingly good characteristic, like fair-mindedness, and you highly value that quality yourself. There is a chance that you will judge many other traits of this particular client as better than they actually are. This is an illustration of the halo effect. On the other hand, if a client has one outstanding negative trait, like closed-mindedness, and you are not a fan of this trait, it is likely to cast a shadow on all other client characteristics. This is the devil effect.

Assessments and clinical decisions based only on the most available information will tend to be biased. They bypass the larger picture. For example, in the past, it was observed that many counselors made a diagnosis based on what they considered one available and striking feature of problem drinking. A recent author noted that a sure sign of alcoholism is being arrested for driving under the influence. That is undeniably a sweeping statement, and anyone who takes it as as the truth is committing an availability error.

Many drivers who are arrested for driving under the influence do indeed have problems with alcohol, but others do not. The latter group do not make it a habit of drinking and driving, do not use alcohol to cope, and exhibit few, if any, signs of problematic drinking. These individuals react poorly to the drug and alcohol education provided in the mandated driving-under-the-influence classes if they are diagnosed as alcoholic within the first five minutes of the class.

These illustrations are at the person-to-person level. What about at a wider level? For example, publishing material not perceived as congruent with the prevailing models of the day has always been a problem in any field. Manuscripts sent to a publisher or journal must go through a peer or editorial review. While the review is often stringent and rational, it is not always so. If the reviewers of a manuscript adhere to a certain point of view and the manuscript is critical of that view, you can expect the reviewers to be critical of the manuscript (the devil effect). On the other hand, if the manuscript is reviewed by those who favor a certain view and the manuscript is supportive of that view, the manuscript is more likely to pass the review.

So, as Sutherland (1994) explains, if you want to avoid these thinking errors:

1. Do not make judgments based on a single piece of information or symptom, no matter how striking it is.
2. Aim to make judgments without halo or devil effects.
3. Try to give an equal amount of weight not only to what you recently learned, but to other information and education.

Obey or Else

Another perception-related irrational thinking fallacy is *obedience*. Some people tend to obey a request or order without much insight as to why. If you doubt this idea, you need to be reminded of the interesting experiment that was conducted at Yale University by Stanley Milgram in the early '60s. Milgram and his colleagues had a number of people, from all walks of life, take part in an experiment that was investigating the effects of punishment on learning. These people were told to administer a series of shocks to subjects who were really part of the experimental team. Each time subjects missed a word they were supposed to learn they were to be administered a shock. The people first watched the subjects, who were strapped into chairs, and were paid $4 for their time. A meter that ranged from 15 to 450 volts was placed in front of the "punishers" and they were instructed to increase the voltage for each miss. Of course, the whole thing was rigged so that no one was really shocked. In addition, the subjects were instructed to miss many of the words. The results were interesting. Of the first set of forty people, twenty-five punishers raised the shock to the 450-volt level. And while there are certainly many ramifications to this old research, it does serve one thing. Some people do as they are told without much questioning.

In the heyday of confronting clients (still evident in places) many counselors would engage in particularly noxious forms of confrontation. This included calling clients names, screaming at them at the top of their lungs, or, swearing at them. When asked why that form of "therapy" was allowed to occur, the often heard answer was, "That's how this program does therapy." Obviously, this standard uncritical answer indicates a high level of obedience to the way the program conducted its treatment.

Programs using this form of obedience prompted certain counselors to act as role models for the rest. One example was a man who had a particularly deep and intimidating voice. You could hear him yelling at his clients even if your office door, down the hall, was closed. Other counselors were encouraged to emulate this style and all new counselors were expected to follow his lead. Most did so without the least questioning. Counselors who did question this form of "therapy," were considered to be soft and were told that they were not suited for this line of work. Those who repeatedly questioned were eventually called into the supervisor's office and often sent home packing. The other counselors continued the noxious confrontations.

Another form of this obedience is sometimes seen in the field. In confidence, many counselors have disclosed that the disease model and how it was applied to clients was sometimes inappropriate. In such programs, clandestine meetings were held because many counselors were afraid they might lose their jobs if they were to speak their minds on this or other entrenched ideas in the field. Obey or leave was the overriding message.

Several students disclosed that in job interviews if they did not say they adhered to the disease model they were not hired. Unfortunately, this adhering to the precepts of the disease model as the only model to be used in a program has tarnished the model's overall effects. The disease model was never intended to be something to be adhered to without question. But, in the minds of many it became dogma and once so, it was something to be obeyed.

To offset this irrational form of thinking:

1. Think critically before you obey. (We add a small caveat to this rule. In today's addiction treatment if you question the philosophy of a program you may become the victim of some level of segregation and distance from your fellow workers, especially, if they are of the obeying nature and you are not.) So be prepared.
2. Question if a command is justified, especially if it is to confront a client noxiously. You have the right and ethical obligation not to permit this form of "therapy."

Do the Accepted Thing

The next irrational thinking form that clouds perception is *conformity.* This has several elements in common with obeying. One such element has to do with fear. As we noted above, not conforming to a program philosophy is bound to alienate the nonconformist. The experience of alienation can easily turn to anxiety and fear. Those emotions then sometimes bring about conforming behaviors in order to lessen the negative feelings.

Another element associated with conformity is the desire to blend in with one's peers or culture. If individuals stopped conforming to the laws and norms of the land, utter chaos would ensue. Imagine a culture in which drivers would not stop at intersections, and planes would take off and land when they please, as simple examples. Some level of conformity is needed in all societies.

Yet, conforming too much can be uncritical and even harmful. For example, once you begin to sustain a certain belief about anything, there is a human tendency to associate only with those who hold the same view. Rarely do you find those who have dissimilar views cavorting together. This is evident in government (Republicans and Democrats), formal religious organizations (Christian evangelicals and Muslims), or addiction studies (advocates of the disease model and those who advocate addiction as a habit). In such cases one side is unwilling to listen to what the other has to say.

One can become so entrenched in a belief, especially if that belief has been made public, that any contrary ideas are regarded as a challenge and only strengthen one's conviction. If challenged, they will try to justify their position, and often do it with relish. This is what happens to many authors in addiction studies. They publish a position, and once the inevitable criticism arrives, they spend a good deal of their careers defending the original position. Just look back through many of the national addiction magazines and journals to see the evidence.

The metaphor of war has been used to describe the "hot debates" (disease vs. non-disease) in the addiction field. One side often vilifies the other as something demonic that is bound to lead the field into ruin.

History is replete with these types of situations. When Freud, for example, began to publish his ideas about human sexuality at a time in which it was not fashionable to even talk about the subject, he received an onslaught of criticism. It could be said that he went on the defensive at this point, and rarely thereafter demonstrated original ideas. He was too busy holding off his critics. This stole much energy from his ability to discover new things. Even worse, he began to use his ideas to criticize his critics. That is, he would label his critics as in a state of repressed sexuality if they published a stinging account against him.

The same thing happens in the addiction field. Key points of a belief are used to explain the motivation of the critic. An opponent can be seen to be in denial, suffering from a childhood trauma that distorts present perceptions, or is in the grip of some irrational thought. You can always criticize a critic using your own pet perspective.

Which Way Do I Go?

The jump to defensiveness is also fueled by *cognitive dissonance* (Festinger, 1957). In this case, one feels a heightened level of discomfort or confusion when one's beliefs are challenged by opposing beliefs. We all like to believe we are intelligent and rational. Yet, when two opposing thoughts come together we feel annoyance and an unpleasant psychological tension. Many will scramble to stabilize this state.

This tension often makes people defensive. In order to lessen it many will resort to their favorite fallacies and mind tunnels. The use of such devices reduces the importance, if not the value, of the conflicting belief. By their uncritical nature, fallacies and mind tunnels can allow a person to stabilize an original belief, while making him/her feel rational, if not right.

The point of this discussion is to demonstrate that conformity can be a strong influence on us. We go to great lengths to support what is dear to us. In the addiction field, we have noxiously confronted many clients "in good faith" in the past out of conformity. All of this was thought to be in the best interests of the client. We watched the so-called experts, were duly impressed, and imitated their behavior. Experts can do that—impress us. However, in these instances, they were disastrously wrong. Experts can also be wrong, especially if they owe allegiance to a certain belief. However, someone who achieves a "name" in the addiction field accrues followers who will conform to the expert's ideas without much critical thinking.

If your colleagues buy into an expert's theories and you don't, you can become the victim of the "crowd mentality." If your peers wholeheartedly accept a new, irrational belief, you have two options. You can either conform in order not to feel out of place, or face the scorn of the crowd mentality. Taking no action is often a sign of conformity.

To defend against this irrational form of thinking, try the following:

1. If you plan on publishing, think your position through. You may find it hard to change it once it is in print.
2. Ask yourself if you believe something just because it conforms to the ideas of your peers, or if you have critically thought the process thorough.
3. Avoid being stampeded by the force of the crowd. Waiting for a calmer moment to reflect might be a wiser move.
4. Try not to be overly impressed by experts. You also have a mind. Use it.
5. If you have made a public pronouncement and it turns out to be inaccurate, change your mind in public. Changing one's mind is a sign of rationality, not weakness.

It's Us or Them

The next perceptual irrational thought fallacy concerns the effects of *belonging to a group*. In the last section, we noted how an individual's behavior tends to conform to what a group thinks. Here we discuss uncritical thinking that can result from belonging to a group.

It makes sense that a group, with its different biases and opinions, would tend to drift toward a position in which the various biases would even out. Right? Wrong! If a group has an established bias to begin with, it tends to become even more biased over time (Sutherland, 1994). The preconceptions a group takes on can be more than the sum of its individual members' preconceptions. Furthermore, it appears as a group thinks (even extreme types of thoughts), so will all its members. A group tries to elicit approval of its actions from its members. In the case of addiction staff meetings, if the majority believes in a concept such as codependency, then the predisposition is set, and the position tends to become more ingrained in that group. In this case, and regardless of other evidence, codependency will become more entrenched in the diagnosis of clients. Those who have different beliefs about this issue may well find their evidence suppressed. In fact, counterarguments may actually strengthen the codependency idea rather than leading to scientific examination. Even if others in the group do not believe in the concept, they will often be afraid to speak out for fear of losing membership (belonging) in the group. This example should give us pause to think of how clinical decisions are sometimes made in treatment program staff meetings.

Janis (1983) called this tendency of groups to drift to extremes *groupthink*. Do not confuse it with critical thinking. In groupthink, groups are overly optimistic, ignore opposing facts, and hold stereotypical views of outsiders. Members tend to silence dissidents, and other members suppress their own doubts regarding a group decision in order to conform. In such an atmosphere, little if any critical thought takes place. Many a clinical addiction decision might be made under irrational conditions (Taleff, 1997).

One can also see this kind of thinking in large addition-oriented organizations. There was a time when ideas other than the disease model, twelve-step recovery, and a disregard for formal academic training would not be allowed a say in these organizations. Not long ago I presented some ideas on the effects of graduate training and the addiction field to a national organization. I indicated that academic training would one day be the basis of education for future addiction clinicians. I pointed out how the early generation of addiction professionals thought, and how the current generation would think differently—more critically, among other things. Following the presentation, a member of the board approached me and stated, "You know what you said here today could not have been said a few years ago." "Yes," I said, "a few years ago I would not have been invited to say the things I did, and I would have probably been booed out of the room." A prime example of groupthink.

Under the influence of groupthink, outsiders are seen in negative terms. They are treated with intolerance and stereotyped. A bias begins to form in the perception of an out-group, and is likely to grow inside the in-group. Even when a person is not physically in a group, that person will carry the bias of the group to most all other interactions.

It is difficult to take pride in any group without regarding outsiders as inferior. Labeling something as inferior (such as an outside opinion) encourages seeing only what we want to see, and dismissing any incompatible opinions outright.

Finally, many groups do not want to think critically. That requires effort, and consensus is rarely reached, thus fostering frustration, among other things. What most groups like to do is take action based on what sticks in their minds (what is available). This is far easier to do.

It is easy to be caught up in groupthink, be it at a staff meeting or in a national organization. To defend against this fallacy:

1. Be cautious and think through the prevailing views of groups, staff meetings, and national organizations.
2. If you are in such a group, ask yourself if opposing views are given a voice and tolerated.
3. Ask yourself how open-minded you are to ideas that oppose your most cherished beliefs.
4. Be very vigilant about stereotypes; they can seep into a belief system almost without notice.

Insight Problems

There is a societal belief that if one can understand a problem, that understanding will solve the problem (Levy, 1997). For example, just because someone has a heart condition and understands what circumstances contribute to that condition does not mean he or she will solve that problem. By the same token, there is little evidence that understanding an addiction solves it.

This is a fallacy committed by many addiction professionals. For example, some counselors persist in pushing clients to dig deeper and deeper into themselves in the hope that such insight will eventually solve their problem. More inventories and diaries are prescribed, and therapy is extended far beyond need.

Now insight has its place. It helps to know what's wrong with a person, and it provides comfort to demystify problems. Yet, there are also drawbacks (Levy, 1997). As stated, utilizing insight too much can lead to excessive internal searching, which can further lead to intellectualization and rationalizing. In this case, behavior is not changed, only excused with another "deeper" elucidation. To address this bias, recognize that insight has its limits, and actively look for alternative methods to induce change.

A Little Too Steady

The last perceptional irrationality in this section is *misplaced consistency.* This fallacy has close associations with the first irrationality we examined: availability. In this case, people strive to maintain consistency despite any opposing facts. There is a strong tendency to exaggerate the good points of a belief and minimize its bad points. In addition, if the presenting points of a counterargument are not understood, or understood and still not accepted, there is a tendency to lower one's opinion of the counterargument, otherwise known as "sour grapes." This is sometimes seen in the addiction field. Many counselors and programs have made large investments in the unitary model of alcoholism (Patterson, Sobel, & Sobel, 1977). Essentially, this model says that alcoholism is a primary, progressive, chronic disease. Yet, when its proponents are presented with evidence that refutes some of these ideas, they will be angered, if not outraged, at such evidence. What one often hears as a rebuttal is, "My personal experience tells me otherwise." An even better one repeatedly heard is, "I never did understand that stuff. Anyway, I don't care what the scientists say, I know what I know." These, among others, are examples of a blatant disregard for the facts, driven by a misplaced consistency that skews thinking.

Closed minds continue to dispense their own brand of therapy even if the empirical support is shaky. This can only harm the client and waste shrinking health dollars that are better spent in other ideas and interventions.

To defend against this mind tunnel:

1. Always be cautious of overrating any opinion or belief you (or others) hold to be accurate and factual. This is particularly true if you have made a large investment in the position.
2. If the evidence starts to refute your position, stop defending it, cut your losses, and change your opinion. An inability to acknowledge your own errors can cost you in terms of critical mistakes in treatment strategies and money.

FALLACIES RELATED TO MANNER AND STYLE

We all have our own style, be it in our walk, our talk, and even our professional life. These styles make us individuals. Most of us seldom pause to reflect on our personal behaviors, language, or even how we go about thinking because these behaviors and thinking habits usually serve us well. Our way of thinking has a familiar feel and comfort level. However, this comfort can have a blinding effect in that we become hardened into believing the way we think is good when maybe it isn't so hot. If our thinking styles turn into concrete we, as professional people, are in trouble.

We will now examine a few manners and styles that cause critical thinking problems. Some of these are sprinkled with the authority bias we encountered a few chapters ago.

A Little Too Much Confidence

The first style we discuss is *overconfidence*. Confidence is fine, but too much of it leads to cockiness. Becoming cocky will certainly bias our ability to judge situations accurately. An overconfident individual rarely seeks out facts to back up a claim.

For example, we humans are adept at making causal, or connecting one thing to another types of explanations for what has happened, after the fact (Sutherland, 1994). This is particularly easy to do with clients who have either relapsed or begun a quality recovery after they have left your program. We can say we predicted either the relapse or continued recovery and thereby fuel our self-confidence.

The problem is that we often make a wrong prediction before the fact. Weeks later, we forget that prediction. The interesting part is that once we hear what has actually happened to a client, we can easily fit the outcome to correspond to our present attitude and perception. That is, we select evidence that will be supportive of any prediction we offer, remembered or not, and we can become cocky about this flawed prediction.

Some addiction professionals can easily build a causal story to explain why their judgment was correct. (When this occurs in our clients, counselors often refer to it as intellectualizing. When it occurs with us, we call it good intuition.) Our memories are not all that accurate to begin with, so distorting what we predicted in the past is easy. There are few around to refute what we really said in the first place, and if there are, they will probably resort to a selective remembering process themselves, thus raising their level of confidence to a higher level than it deserves.

This kind of overconfidence can have significant repercussions in addiction treatment. For example, members of a treatment team could easily deceive themselves into thinking they were doing a terrific job with a population of clients when, in fact, they were not. Shrinking health money could conceivably be spent on useless interventions. In short, the confidence placed in certain strategies is unwarranted.

One last problem with overconfidence is that more knowledge may not necessarily raise credibility but may just add to overconfidence (Piattelli-Palmarini, 1994). Studies have noted that when psychologists and students were given more information about the history of a real client they tended to be unable to discriminate among statements about the client accurately (Sutherland, 1994). The only thing to increase was their confidence to assess the case.

This same scenario can be seen in a host of addiction professional staff meetings across the country. In many instances, it has been observed that any additional information obtained on a client is simply used to support a pre-judgmental disposition or theory.

Recommendations to neutralize overconfidence include:

1. Never trust predictions made after the fact.
2. To combat your own propensity to overconfidence, try to find evidence or arguments that are incompatible with your opinions and beliefs.
3. If you really want to test your predictive abilities, start writing them down. Give a copy to a trusted colleague and then compare your prediction to what really happened and be prepared to eat lots of crow.

My Gut Told Me So

The next fallacy focuses on *human intuition*. We discussed parts of this fallacy before but it deserves its own section. Intuition is an instinctive hunch by which we respond to subtle cues and assemble bits of data, like a jigsaw puzzle, into something greater than its parts (Nichell, 2005).

Sutherland (1994) and Dawes (1994) have studied our intuition and found it remarkably inaccurate. In fact, when compared to formal mathematical analysis, the judgments of math are much better than the judgments of people (Sutherland, 1994). This has profound implications as to assessments and treatment strategies conducted on clients with addiction problems, not to mention the predictive abilities of addiction professionals.

Yet, many in our field swear by their intuition. They say "I knew he was going to relapse all along. My feelings told me so." Or, "I always trust my gut." (Never mind that they never once did a retrogressive analysis of those feelings to test their accuracy.)

Reasons for inaccuracy include the fact that the construction of any intuition requires memory. Memory is not precise and is notoriously influenced by misinformation, dubious testimonials, and the propensity to perceive connections where none exist (Myers, 2004). Thus, intuition is often related more to confidence than to accuracy. If it feels right, then for all practical purposes it *is* right.

It is remarkable, in this day and age, how people mistrust figures and reliable statistical analysis compared to their own intuition. But what's wrong with intuition? First, human judgment does not assign an optimal set of standards to the things predicted. As we have seen, if something is personally valued, it is that value that will carry weight in a judgment. Depending on our personal preferences, we will assign inappropriate value to certain information. Second, most people are not good at combining different pieces of information. When presented with a client case in which there are a number of opposing segments of data (i.e., interview information that is different from instrument-obtained information) they will frequently rely on their intuition rather than other, more reliable sources of information. In some cases, they do not assign any value at all to their assessments. This can be seen in the lack of credence many counselors give to reliable test results. The third reason intuition is so unreliable is that a counselor's mood and disposition will vary from day to day. This cannot help but influence assessment and treatment interventions. Fourth is the ever-present availability influence—our tendency to rely on what is recently available in our memory bank. Fifth are the multitude of types and sources of information available on a client (e.g., demographics, diagnosis, character traits, personal history and development, etc.). That collection of information may be too much for any one addiction professional to handle and put into proper perspective. The sixth is the conjunction effect, where we find it easier to imagine what is more probable and familiar to us (Piattelli-Palmarini, 1994). Anything outside that characteristic style is discarded as a possible alternative. This particular way of seeing the world is sure to obscure any individual qualities about a client.

Two more issues add to the feeling that one's intuition is factual. One is the notion that most of us want to believe that we have special skills and talents when it comes to judging our fellow humans. After all, haven't we been trained to do that, and haven't we accumulated years of experience in this field?

Furthermore, the idea of mathematics being so much more accurate than we are is unnerving to many of us. How are formulas supposed to account for the unexpected? Formulas don't have souls, and only humans can understand humans. Thus, goes the illogic, all the more reason to trust the "gut."

Recommendations to address the supposed accuracy of intuition include the following:

1. Be very wary of counselors who say they have an accurate "feel" about people. Instead, ask to see any empirical evidence they have accumulated on how accurate their intuition/gut really is.
2. If you are a professional in the addiction field and you don't understand statistical analysis and its predictive abilities, it's time to learn them.
3. If you still think you have special talents in judging people, and it turns out to be true by virtue of rigorous empirical analysis collected over the years, write a book and teach the rest of us.

Stage Presence

Few addiction professionals would deny that our field has its share of individuals who have a pleasing voice, an air of sincerity about them, or a certain level of attractiveness. Such people can be found in videotapes, workshops, and staff meetings. They are a charismatic bunch to be sure, but that style is often their downfall because much of what they say impresses with heart-rending stories and little else.

As noted, a fair share of these workshop trainers and authors use *emotive words* or *false analogies* to fill an audience with strong emotions. What's wrong with that? Nothing, if ahead of time the speaker announces that what is to follow is exactly that—an evening of inspirational sermons. But if a speaker leaves the audience with the impression that his/her presentation is somehow linked to the royal road to the truth, then we have a serious problem.

Such presentations obscure rationality and have very little critical thinking behind them. Audience members were observed to exit of one of these showy encounters with lavish praise for the inspirational and moving speaker. However, upon further questioning, these same people could not recall a single bit of tangible information to bring back to their clients. In the end, audience members shelled out $200 for an evening of slick, emotion-laden mush.

In the same vein is the fallacy that *bold statements make claims true*. Just because something is said with conviction does not make it factual. A treatment program representative who makes a claim that what the program conducts is the most successful approach to recovery is making a bold statement and an extraordinary claim. It is incumbent on that program or treatment strategy to supply proof for the claim. In addition, not only must the program supply proof of its efficacy, it must also convince others of the validity of that proof. To date, no such extraordinary proof of success exists for any program or strategy in our field.

To offset these tactics:

1. Keep both feet firmly planted on scientific and verifiable ground.
2. Ask questions either in your mind or directly to the presenter for empirically based evidence to any claims he/she may have made.
3. Remember that critical thinkers can be as emotional as the next person, but they generally will not use emotion to sway the minds of others.

Thinking or making decisions while under the influence of strong emotions is asking for trouble. There is convincing evidence that emotional distress can impinge on mental clarity (Goleman,

1995). Strong emotions prevent people and addiction counselors from thinking well.

Consider a life-and-death crisis in your program. One of your clients has attempted suicide while in your facility. You receive a call late at night to come to the emergency room of your local hospital. On the drive over, all sorts of things go through your head. You can feel your heart pumping and your hands trembling. Upon arrival, you are trying to make rational decisions, but nothing comes out right. Under these conditions, the working memory of your brain is being overwhelmed, and it holds all relevant information to the task at hand. Without that information, there is no way you are going to be doing any critical thinking. Energy is too invested in other activities.

The emotion does not have to be acute to interfere with thinking. Chronic, long-term stress can also distort thinking and decision making. Stress can effect memory, reasoning ability, flexibility in thought, and can elicit feelings of depression. The addiction counselor needs crisp thinking in his/her daily work. Yet, chronic stress can cause the counselor to rely on routine, non-individualized treatment strategies. Fixed ways of thinking tend to solidify under stress. Routine strategies create resistance in a client because they reduce the client to the routine and miss the unique aspects of each individual.

Attempting to use a run-of-the-mill technique across the board on clients will sooner or later invite resistance from everyone involved. The addiction counselor will expect a client to respond positively to a routine treatment intervention. When the proper response doesn't come, the frustrated counselor may use the routine strategy of confrontation, with its accompanying negative emotions. As the evidence indicates, this doesn't work (Miller & Rollnick, 1991).

To address strong emotions and the subsequent problems with thinking:

1. Delay making any critical decisions while under the influence of strong emotions or chronic stress, especially if they concern a counseling situation.
2. Know a few techniques in relaxation training you can use when needed.
3. Take some time and consult with your supervisor or a trusted colleague.

CHAPTER SUMMARY

Perception Fallacies

- The perceptions of addiction counselors can cause critical thinking problems.
- A major perception error is using only what is most available in your mind to make clinical decisions.
- Another error is to favor (or disfavor) certain traits and allow that perception to influence a clinical decision.
- Too much unquestioning obedience to anything, especially addiction ideas, is asking for trouble.
- Like obedience, too much conformity is asking for trouble.
- Belonging to a group has its value, but not at the cost of critical thinking.
- Just because you understand (have insight into) a problem in no way solves it.
- Being steady and consistent is admirable, but flat out wrong if valuable information is dismissed.

Manner and Style Fallacies

- Although convenient and often accurate, our personal style and manner, if not periodically evaluated, can solidify so that we believe we assess and judge better than we do. Once that happens, we will make mistakes in counseling.
- Overconfidence is a fallacy of style that says we assess and judge well when in fact we don't.
- Believing that fallible human intuition is more accurate than it is creates clinical problems.
- Emotional words, false analogies, and bold statements convey little in the way of good, solid evidence.
- Thinking or making decisions while under the influence of strong emotions will generate clinical nightmares.

CHAPTER TWELVE

The Ethics and Professional Consequences of Using Critical Thinking

By now you have achieved an understanding of critical thinking. That has been the whole point of this book. You now grasp the essentials of a good argument and some reasons people resort to bad thinking. You have reviewed many fallacies that addiction professionals fall prey to, as well as a number of methods to avoid such pitfalls. But with all this new understanding comes some caution and ethical reflection.

To be blunt, you have in your hands a most powerful set of tools. They need to be used with care and respect. Powerful tools, like anything powerful, have a tendency to corrupt. They can make opponents look worse than they are and lead one to deeply humiliate another. That is *not,* I repeat, *not* the goal of critical thinking. The following questions may serve as a set of broad guidelines to offset this corrupting propensity. They were adapted from Brookfield (1987) and Hughes (2000). For example:

- Is it right to attack weakness in plain view of others?
- How far should we go to reveal the weakness in others' arguments?
- How far should we go in revealing our weakness to our opponents?
- We need to be fair to our opponents. How can we do that?

- Should we resort to distortion in order to win an argument?
- How forceful should we be in our attempt to persuade others to agree with our views?

ALTRUISM BEGINS AT HOME

Hughes (2000) suggests that we utilize the principle of charity when we respond to arguments. This principle is simple and just requires us to treat our opponents fairly. In the public forum, we give them an opportunity to clarify what they have said. When they are not present, we adopt a generous interpretation of their ideas. In other words, we do what we can to avoid demeaning the argument or the person, or fall into a critical thinking fallacy that only gives us a superficial sense of gratification. As always, we are looking for the most reasonable explanation for an argument.

Although some believe that the whole point of a debate or argument is to win, it is clearly to move closer to some truth. Those who have witnessed debates where fallacies are heaped upon the opposition, along with an unhealthy dose of name calling, can attest to the fact that this is not the way to evolve and advance addiction facts.

ADDITIONAL RECOMMENDATIONS

The following are additional suggestions that are useful when engaging in ethical critical thinking arguments. They are meant to facilitate critical thinking without abuse, and were adapted from Brookfield (1987).

Affirm and Respect Others

Critical thinking in the addiction field should not be used to threaten the integrity of others. This includes the blatant disregard of people's feelings with insults and out and out condemnation of their ideas. Even small signs, such as a raised eyebrow, a smirk of distain, or a look of superiority can threaten someone's ego. Such immature behavior is certain to drive people into a defensive posture and close down clear thinking. One needs to walk a delicate line between respecting a thinker's integrity and posing challenging questions.

Listen Attentively

Listening in an attentive and respectful fashion allows one to recognize overt and covert comments that cover up powerful assumptions and critical thinking fallacies. Respectful listening allows one to frame questions that are fair and easily understood. Not listening only furthers the predisposition to jump to conclusions and make unfounded assumptions.

Be a Critical Thinking Teacher

As one who understands critical thinking, you now have an obligation, as ideas are circulated in our field, to be a catalyst for in-depth discussion and critical inquiry. One major obligation is to nurture and encourage new ideas and dreams. Quiet reflection is a start in this direction.

There is also an obligation to fight propaganda, unfounded ideas, and malice. That means challenging advertisements, books, and workshops that contain harmful and patently wrong information.

Remember, a critical thinker needs to be humble. Please do not fall into the temping role of the omniscient guru of critical thinking.

One last item in this category.

The Virtues of a Closed Mind

Critical thinking has its share of naysayers who will present predictable arguments. One favorite is that critical thinkers close their minds to many things. To that I answer with a hearty, "Yes! To some ideas, critical thinkers do have closed minds and are proud of it."

You should close your mind to certain things as tightly as possible. In fact, you have an ethical obligation to close your mind to certain claims, especially to demonstrably incorrect ones (Huber, 1991). Civilization no longer burns witches because science has closed its mind to the belief that certain women and men cause plagues, pestilence, and crop blight. Yet, sadly, even today one hears reports of certain regions in the world where people are held responsible for the lack of rain and subsequently punished. Critical thinkers close their minds to that type of claim.

Critical thinkers close their mind to the idea that a woman should be stoned for adultery or genitally mutilated. We close our minds to claims that natural disasters (e.g., tsunamis, hurricanes) are earned punishment for human sin. We close our minds to TV programs that promote the idea that one can communicate with the dead to receive communiqués from the beyond. We close our minds to gang raping a female family member so that a family's pride can be somehow salvaged. We close our minds to pet psychics who purport to give messages to animals' owners. We close our minds to disenfranchising certain cultures for financial gain or power. We close our minds to aborting baby girls because the prevailing culture favors male babies. We close our minds to slavery in all its forms.

Closer to the addiction field, we close our minds to harsh confrontational tactics that claim a goal of honesty at the cost of derogation and humiliation. We close our minds to gouging insurance companies just because a client has additional coverage. We close our minds to untested and unproven counseling techniques. We close our minds to padding records in order to pass a state or national licensing survey. We close our minds to graduate students who do not get hired in programs because they are not personally recovering. We close our minds to programs and counselors who dismiss valuable research because the data do not fit a favored pet theory. And, we close our minds to efforts to slow the process of bringing modern science into the addiction field.

We also close our minds to solving clinical problems with reason alone. Reason without the balance of kindness, compassion, and humanity can create false beliefs (Peat, 2003). History has shown us that these types of beliefs can lead to all sorts of justifications that burn, lynch or torture innocent people.

WHAT PRICE CRITICAL THINKING?

At the risk of creating a straw man, there are certain cautions, to be considered when using critical thinking on yourself, with your colleagues, and in the field in general.

Feeling Alone

If you have learned anything about critical thinking in our field, I hope it has been that the process requires you to step out of the mainstream of addiction thought and belief. In fact, it forces you to step out of any pet ideas you have and almost everything you've ever learned, and not to assume that there is only one world out there and only one way to think about it (Moldoveanu & Langer, 2002). This posture of questioning things upsets certain people. Stepping out from the mainstream usually does.

However, the addiction field has had its share of pretty bizarre ideas over the years. Critical thinking is being promoted as an effort to challenge such ideas. If we don't confront them, they will surely flourish. Such a stance only leads people to accept nonsense. With such unquestioning acceptance comes intellectual stagnation.

Yet, as we know, the price for stepping out and challenging certain beliefs is isolation and loneliness, which come in a variety of forms. Some colleagues may begin to avoid you at the lunch table, or wait for the next elevator if you are on it because they don't want to be seen associating with you. Why?

As pointed out, most of us do not like having our ideas confronted even though there might be solid, credible evidence for such a confrontation. After years of experience, a certain level of self-pride often sets in that makes it difficult for professional addiction counselors to handle criticism well. We like to rest in cozy complacency (Blackburn, 1999).

However, critical thinking teaches you to swallow your pride. Sooner or later you will be confronted with a competent argument and/or evidence to challenge a favored idea. If you are a critical thinker, deep down you will know you are wrong, and will go about changing. That's the happy ending version. The other, more real-life ending is the one in which we don't want to be seen as wrong and end up fighting ugly battles and making enemies.

Although constructively criticizing a "toe the line" philosophy often results in some degree of isolation, a positive element to this isolation is that deep inside you know that your questions will bring clarity to your clinical and administrative work. The result is better treatment for all your clients.

One more thing: Isolation and loneliness may come about because the critical thinker moves away from trivial and uncritical types of conversation. This distancing can be seen as arrogance (I am better than you because I think). However, the distancing comes from the desire not to "play the game" any more and not from arrogance. The game is a tolerance of sloppy thinking. Rather than engage in such thinking, which creates hurt feelings, the more civil move is to gain some distance from others who do. Criticism, no matter how gentle or well meaning, does not often stop people from thinking poorly and more often than not it agitates. Then a defensive posture results. Now we have bitterness and acrimony between addiction professionals, which contributes nothing to professional or personal development. Sometimes it is best to let things ride and wait for better opportunities to engage others.

Anger

As noted in the first chapter, many believe that a substantial investment in critical thinking will begin to wear on one's ability to empathize with others or that it will undermine your faith or show you that life is hopeless (Mole, 2002). The price for critical thinking is the frustration you may experience with these persistent fallacies and uncritical thinking myths. The frustration will often provoke anger.

A suggested means of dealing with the hot emotions of anger and frustration is to channel them into the "cool cognitive," as espoused by Ayduk and Mischel (2002). The cool pursuits of writing and developing reasoned causes are an excellent way to transform this hot energy. There are a number of writing venues from which to choose. They include writing pieces for popular addiction magazines, conducting research for journal articles, and even writing books about critical thinking and the addiction profession. That is how much of this book got written.

One Last Price to Pay

The price of critical thinking will not always come from without but sometimes from within. There is a level of awareness and deep reflection that develops from years of critical thinking (Pigliucci, 2000). Although awareness seems inviting, if not desirable, it can be somewhat unsettling. The greater your awareness the more it tends to make you different.

This awareness is not a simple accumulation of facts. Rather it has a number of features (Troxell & Synder, 1976). For example, it includes assimilating ideas that stand in stark contrast to your usual way of making sense of the world. The world changes constantly. This constant change takes getting used to, making moving from one plane of understanding to another disconcerting. If you don't like change, then the growing level of awareness is all the more unsettling.

Greater awareness allows you to focus on those aspects of the world that are different. The evolution of the addiction field has brought about many changes in treatment methods and thinking. Those changes came at the price of anguish and toil. Some people ended up looking good, whereas others looked foolish.

No individual can arrive at a true personal or professional philosophy without discarding much that he/she would have preferred to keep, and accepted much that he/she would have rather discarded (Stewart & Blocker, 1982).

The long and hard argument made in this book is that critical thinking will give you perspective and improve your thinking. Yet, be warned that there is a price to pay.

CHAPTER SUMMARY

- When engaging in a debate utilize the principle of charity. Simply, be kind to the person with whom you argue.
- When you take on an argument with others affirm and respect them, listen attentively, and be a critical thinking addiction studies teacher.
- There are certain virtues to having a closed mind.

Feeling alienated and alone, angered by the thinking of others, and maintaining your own equilibrium may well be prices to pay for becoming a critical thinker. However, the payoff is extraordinary. Not only will your clinical, administrative, and supervisory decisions improve, which will certainly benefit your clients; but critical thinking will let you spread your wings, and experience the electrifying thrill of clear new thoughts.

Glossary

accommodation process: a process whereby we modify our thinking to fit the facts.

ad hominem fallacy: criticizes the person, not the argument.

after this, therefore because of this fallacy (post hoc, ergo propter hoc, or a false cause): believing that just because something occurred before an event it was that something that caused the event.

appeal to authority fallacy: wants you to believe that just because some people are supposedly experts, then what they say is accurate.

appeal to force fallacy: enduring pressure, be it economic, physical, or other forms of influence, to sway an argument.

appeal to ignorance (ad ignorantiam): assumes that in some mysterious way the absence of evidence supports something as true.

appeal to the many fallacy: gains its influence from consensus, and the belief that because everybody is doing it, it is the right thing to do.

appeal to pity fallacy: coercion with an emotional twist (feel sorry for me).

appeal to tradition or folk wisdom: similar to the appeal to authority, but in this case the appeal is not to a person, but to a doctrine.

argument: a set of claims designed to settle a main point.

assimilation bias: seeing the world through our own set of schema-colored glasses.

assimilation process: modifying the facts to fit our view of things.

attribution creep: perceiving clients as an example of a preferred counselor theory rather than objectively.

availability error: the tendency to judge something or someone by the first thing that comes to mind, especially right after reading a book or attending a workshop.

basic criteria of a good argument:

> **acceptable:** The premise needs to be true. A false premise cannot provide support for a conclusion.
> **relevant:** Premises need to be related, correlated, and appropriate to the conclusion
> **adequate:** This is a matter of degree. Premises can add very little or a great deal of support to a conclusion.

begging the question: declaring a certainty in premises. The premises turn out to be the conclusion that was desired in the first place.

belonging to a group: mindset where individual thought takes a backseat to prevailing group beliefs.

bi-directionality: a situation in which two events cause one another.

bold statements do not make claims true fallacy: saying something with conviction does not make it factual.

causal fallacies: fallacies that make errors in cause-and-effect reasoning.

claim: a statement that is either true or false.

clarity: To determine this quality in an argument, note the following:

- Is the argument plainly defined?
- Is it understandable?
- Is the presenter trying to win followers, or can he/she supply ample evidence for a conclusion?

classification fallacies: a group of fallacies that muddle the clarity of taxonomy with various levels of ambiguity.

cognitive dissonance: two opposing thoughts coming together can cause annoyance and unpleasant psychological tension. In those uncomfortable times many will scramble for answers and become prone to use fallacies to stabilize their confused state.

complex argument: an argument that has two (or more) related premises and one conclusion.

conclusion: a principal or main point of an argument.

conformity mind tunnel: the tendency to conform, obey, and fall in line with little or no thought.

damn the origin: a fallacy that does not attack a person but attacks the source (journal, newspaper, magazine, etc).

deduction: Traditionally considered as the ideal form of reasoning, it consists of at least two premises (reasons, statements) that are intended to lead to a conclusion. So, if your premises are true, the conclusion that follows will also be true.

devil effect: judging someone or something as worse than it actually is.

dialectic: Socratic questioning where a position is challenged to assess accuracy.

emotional cognition: believing what your feelings say is true.

emotive words and false analogies: the use of strong emotions, symbolic language, touching stories, and little else to sway a person or audience.

equating anecdotes to science: stories and anecdotes used to support certain claims. They are used as "evidence" for scientific data.

exclusive generalizing fallacy: reducing complex information to a simple or singular explanation.

explanation: easily confused with a real argument because it shares a common vocabulary, but only describes a situation. It does not tell you how correct a situation or claim is.

facts: claims that are true or have good evidence or justification.

fallacies: reasoning tricks that try to persuade you to accept something as true when in reality it isn't.

false dichotomy, either-or: fallacy that presumes that there are only two possibilities for a certain condition when in fact there are many.

fundamental attribution error: the tendency to ascribe the actions of people to their personality traits and not to a situation.

group think: a group mindset that ignores facts and stereotypes outsiders.

halo effect: judging someone or something as better than it actually is.

hasty generalization (overgeneralizing): the fallacy that jumps to a conclusion before the facts warrant that conclusion.

human intuition: a mind-tunnel style that relies on unsubstantiated hunches and guesses.

hypothesis: a generalization arrived at through induction.

hypothetical syllogism: combines deduction and induction to form a new syllogism, or a term that says, "If so and so, then so and so."

ignoring the evidence and/or **unrepresentative thinking fallacy:** the tendency to simply neglect information that doesn't agree with a favored theory or idea.

inclusive generalizing fallacy: the fallacy that includes many reasons for defining a claim, but ends up defining nothing specific.

incorrect classification fallacy: process whereby clinicians often misdiagnose/misclassify because of reliance on vague terms, which lead to ambiguous and often incorrect classifications.

inductive: arguments based on research data that do not guarantee some final truth. At best, they can only give high or low probabilities.

inference: asks, even demands, that one thought is supported, justified, or reasonably linked to another.

irrelevant fallacies: distraction from or discrediting information you don't need in an argument.

issue: the focus of a debate, contention, or argument.

logic: that which supports assertions with reasoning. Logic takes us from one point to another in an assured and sensible manner. It is interested in the correctness of a claim, and whether one inference follows another.

making the wrong connection fallacy: believing that one thing causes another when in fact it doesn't.

meme: a mental unit of information or idea that influences behavior andevents; and which can create more copies of itself.

misinterpreting of evidence fallacy: here evidence is misjudged, misunderstood, or misread.

misplaced consistency: the mindset where people strive to maintain a viewpoint despite opposing facts.

mistaking the cause or **misplaced causality fallacy:** error where one assigns a cause to the most conspicuous event available from a number of possible and equally relevant events.

more striking/dramatic the event fallacy: the more vivid an event, the more we are likely to consider it as a cause when other, more reasonable events are more likely to be the cause.

near arguments: features that look like arguments but are not (see reports and explanations).

obedience: the tendency to do as you are told without questioning.

Occam's razor: theories that account for the most information with the fewest assumptions.

odium scholasticum: an attitude of smugness and hubris often seen in academics and demonstrated by belittling statements directed at theories or ideas that do not meet with scientific approval.

opinions: beliefs and attitudes, which are often accepted as true.

overcommitment to an ideology: too much dedication to a belief or idea.

overconfidence: a mind-tunnel style that converts normal confidence into cockiness.

personal interaction fallacy: the belief that if I had personal experiences with an addiction or other problem, then someone else's addiction or problem has the same cause.

premises: reasons and/or facts for accepting a conclusion.

primal thinking: egocentric, selfish thinking.

qualification: a limitation or restriction.

reactivity: the very act of observing, which can affect one's perception.

red herring: the use of any means to draw attention away from the issue at hand.

reification: turning something that has a conceptual base into something that is considered concrete or actual.

representativeness fallacy: the tendency of humans to remember our successes rather than our failures, thus biasing our memory.

reports of arguments: does just what it says it does. It reports that an argument was argued in a certain way and nothing more.

scientific method: theorizing or asking questions to arrive at a higher form of argument. The scientific method contains four essential and repeating steps:

- observe a phenomenon
- form a tentative explanation of cause and effect (theory)
- observe and experiment (or both) to rule out alternative explanations (test)
- refine and retest the explanation.

simple argument: an argument that has one premise and one conclusion.

slippery slope: a fallacy whereby one makes predictions based on some set of chain reactions, which, if set in motion, will result in some dire consequences.

stereotyping: presumes that a certain set of properties is applicable to an entire group.

straw man: falsify a position taken by another person, then attack the false image you just created.

syllogism: a premise-premise-conclusion argument.

thinking or making decisions while under the influence of strong emotions: a mindset whereby powerful emotions impinge on mental clarity.

two wrongs fallacy: points out that the person does not practice what he/she preaches, therefore if you did it, I can too.

vague terms: words or expressions that by there very nature are imprecise even if the context is clear.

v argument: an argument that can have two or more premises, but each premise can stand alone and still make a conclusion. Yet, together, they make for a stronger argument.

warrant: clarifier that notes whether the evidence for a claim is connected to the conclusion.

weak induction fallacies: making errors by not supplying enough evidence to support a conclusion.

References

Adler, A. (1954). *Understanding human nature*. Greenwich, CT: Fawcett, 1927.

Alcock, J. E. (1996). The propensity to believe. In P. R. Gross, N. Levitt, & M. W. Lewis (Eds.), *The flight from science and reason* (pp. 64–78). Baltimore: Johns Hopkins University Press.

Alcock, J. (2001, May/June). Science vs. pseudoscience, nonscience, and nonsense. *Skeptical Inquirer, 25*, 50–54.

Allegretti, C. L. & Frederick, J. N. (1995). A model for thinking critically about ethical issues. *Teaching of Psychology, 22*, 146–148.

Allen, S. (1998). *"Dumbth": The lost art of thinking*. Amherst, NY: Prometheus Books.

Allport, G. (1954). *The nature of prejudice*. Cambridge, MA: Addison-Wesley.

American Psychiatric Association. (1994). *The diagnostic and statistical manual* (4th ed.). Washington DC: Author.

Angelo, T. A. (1995). Classroom assessment for critical thinking. *Teaching of Psychology, 22*, 6–7.

Arnoult, L. H., & Anderson, C. A. (1988). Identifying and reducing causal reasoning bias in clinical practice. In D. C. Turk & P. Salovey (Eds.), *Reasoning, inference, & judgment in clinical psychology* (pp. 209–232). New York: Free Press.

Ayduk, O., & Mischel, W. (2002). When smart people behave stupidly: Reconciling inconsistencies in social-emotional intelligence. In R. J. Sternberg (Ed.), *Why smart people can be so stupid* (pp. 86–105). New Haven, CT: Yale University Press.

Bandman, E. L., & Bandman, B. (1988). *Critical thinking in nursing*. East Norwalk: CT: Appleton & Lange.

Bates, B. (1995). *A guide to critical thinking*. Philadelphia: J. B. Lippincott.

Bauer, H. H. (2001). *Science or pseudoscience: Magnetic healing, psychic phenomena, and other heterodoxies.* Urbana and Chicago: University of Illinois Press.

Beck, A. T. (1999). *Prisoners of hate: The cognitive basis of anger, hostility, and violence.* New York: HarperCollins.

Bensley, D. A. (1998). *Critical thinking in psychology: A unified skills approach.* Pacific Grove, CA: Brooks/Cole.

Blackburn, S. (1999). *Think.* New York: Oxford University Press.

Blackmore, S. (2004). *Consciousness: An introduction.* Oxford, England: Oxford University Press.

Booth, W. C., Colomb, G. G., & Williams, J. M. (1995). *The craft of research.* Chicago: University of Chicago Press.

Bordens, K. S., & Abbott, B. B. (1996). *Research design and method: A process approach.* Mountain View, CA: Mayfield.

Bowell, T., & Kemp, G. (2002). *Critical thinking: A concise guide.* London: Routledge.

Brodie, R. (1996). *Virus of the mind: The new science of the meme.* Seattle, WA: Integral Press.

Bronowski, J. (1978). *The origins of knowledge and imagination.* New Haven, CT: Yale University Press.

Brookfield, S. D. (1987). *Developing critical thinkers: Challenging adults to explore alternative ways of thinking and acting.* San Francisco: Jossey-Bass.

Browne, M. N., & Keeley, S. M. (2004). *Asking the right questions: A guide to critical thinking* (7th ed.). Upper Saddle River, NJ: Pearson/Prentice Hall.

Buelow, G. D., & Buelow, S. A. (1998). *Psychotherapy in chemical dependence treatment: A practical integrative approach.* Pacific Grove, CA: Brooks/Cole.

Burns, D. D. (1980). *Feeling good: The new mood therapy.* New York: Morrow.

Calvin, W. H. (2002). *A brain for all seasons: Human evolution & abrupt climate change.* Chicago: University of Chicago Press.

Cannavo, S. (1998). *Think to win: The power of logic in everyday life.* Amherst, NY: Prometheus Books.

Carlson, E. R. (1995). Evaluating the credulity of sources: A missing link in the treating of critical thinking. *Teaching of Psychology, 22,* 39–41.

Carter, R. (1998). *Mapping the mind.* Berkeley: University of California Press.

Charpak, G., & Broch, H. (2004). *Debunked.* Baltimore and London: Johns Hopkins University Press.

Christian, J. L. (1977). *Philosophy: An introduction to the art of wondering.* New York: Holt, Rinehart and Winston.

Conway, D. A., & Munson, R. (1997). *The elements of reasoning.* Belmont, CA: Wadsworth.

Craig, E. (2002). *Philosophy: A very short introduction.* Oxford, England: Oxford University Press.

Dauer, F. W. (1989). *Critical thinking: An introduction to reasoning.* New York: Barnes & Noble.

Dawes, R. M. (1994). *House of cards: Psychology and psychotherapy built on myth.* New York: Free Press.

Dawkins, R. (1978). *The selfish gene.* Oxford, England: Oxford University Press.

Dewdney, A. K. (1997). *Yes, we have no neutrinos.* New York: Wiley.

Dorner, D. (1989). *The logic of failure.* New York: Metropolitan Books.

Duncan, B. L., Hubble, M. A., & Miller, S. D. (1997). *Psychotherapy with impossible clients: The effective treatment of therapy veterans.* New York: Norton.

Edelman, G. M. (2004). *Wider than the sky.* New Haven, CT: Yale University Press.

Ehrlich, R. (2001). *Nine crazy ideas in science.* Princeton, NJ: Princeton University Press.

Elder, L., & Paul, R. (1997). *Critical thinking: A stage theory.* Santa Rosa, CA: Foundation for Critical Thinking.

Engel, S. M. (1976). *With good reason: An introduction to informal fallacies.* New York: St. Martin's Press.

Ennis, R. H. (1989). Critical thinking and subject specificity: Clarification and needed research. *Educational Researcher, 18,* 13–16.

Estling, R. (2002, November/December). It's a good thing cows can't fly in Mobile. *Skeptical Inquirer, 26*(6), 57–58.

Fearnside, W. W. (1980). *About thinking.* Englewood Cliffs, NJ: Prentice-Hall.

Fearnside, W. W., & Holther, W. B. (1959). *Fallacy: The counterfeit of argument.* Englewood Cliffs, NJ: Spectrum Books.

Festinger, L. (1957). *A theory of cognitive dissonance.* Evanston, IL: Row & Peterson.

Fisher, A. (2001). *Critical thinking: An introduction.* Cambridge, UK: Cambridge University Press.

Fraenkel, J. R., & Wallen, N. E. (2000). *How to design and evaluate research in education.* Boston: McGraw/Hill.

Friedlander, M. W. (1995). *At the fringes of science.* Boulder, CO: Westview.

Gambrill, E. (1990). *Critical thinking in clinical practice.* San Francisco: Jossey-Bass.

Garb, H. N., & Boyle, P. A. (2003). Understanding why some clinicians use pseudoscientific methods: Findings from clinical research. In

S. O. Lilienfeld, S. J. Lynn, & J. M. Lohr (Eds.), *Science and pseudoscience in clinical psychology* (pp. 17–38). New York: Guilford.
Gazzaniga, M.S. (2005). *The ethical brain.* New York: Dana Press
Gibbs, L., & Grambrill, E. (1996). *Critical thinking for social workers: A workbook.* Thousand Oaks, CA: Pine Forge.
Goleman, D. (1995). *Emotional intelligence.* New York: Bantam Books.
Grigorenko, E. L., & Lockery, D. (2002). Smart is as stupid does: Exploring bases of erroneous reasoning of smart people regarding learning and other disabilities. In R. J. Sternberg (Ed.), *Why smart people can be so stupid* (pp. 159–186). New Haven, CT: Yale University Press.
Halonen, J. S. (1995). Demystifying critical thinking. *Teaching of Psychology, 22,* 75–81.
Halpern, D. F. (1998). Teaching critical thinking across domains, dispositions, skills, structure training, and metacognitive monitoring. *American Psychologist, 53,* 449–455.
Halpern, D. F. (2002). Sex, lies, and audiotapes: The Clinton-Lewinsky scandal. In R. J. Sternberg (Ed.), *Why smart people can be so stupid* (pp. 106–123). New Haven, CT: Yale University Press.
Harnadek, A. (1998). *Critical thinking: Book one.* Pacific Grove, CA: Critical Thinking Press & Software.
Hayes, N. (2000). *Doing psychological research: Gathering and analyzing data.* Buckingham, England: Open University Press.
Hoffer, E. (1963). *The ordeal of change.* New York: Harper & Row.
Honer, S. M., & Hunt, T. C. (1968). *Invitation to philosophy: An introductory handbook.* Belmont, CA: Wadsworth.
Hospers, J. (1953). *An introduction to philosophical analysis.* New York: Prentice-Hall.
Huber, P. W. (1991). *Galileo's revenge: Junk science in the courtroom.* New York: Basic Books.
Hughes, W. (2000). *Critical thinking: An introduction to basic skills* (3rd ed.). Peterborough, Ontario, Canada: Broadview.
Hurley, P. J. (1997). *A concise introduction to logic* (6th ed.). Belmont CA: Wadsworth.
Institute of Medicine. (1990). *Broadening the base for alcohol problems.* Washington, DC: National Academy Press.
Janis, I. L. (1983). *Groupthink: Psychological studies of policy in decisions and fiascoes* (2nd ed.). Boston: Houghton Mifflin.
Kerlinger, F. N. (1986). *Foundations of behavioral research* (3rd ed.). Fort Worth, TX: Harcourt Brace College Publishers.
Kowit, S. (2004). The mass suicide of the Xhosa: A study in the collective self-deception. *Skeptic, 11*(1), 52–57.
Kurfiss, J. G. (1988). *Critical thinking: Theory, research, practice, and*

possibilities (ASHE-ERIC Higher Education Report No. 2). Washington, DC: Association for the Study of Higher Education.

Kurland, D. J. (1995). *I know what it says . . . what does it mean?* Belmont, CA: Wadsworth.

Langer, E. J. (1989). *Mindfulness.* Reading, MA: Addison-Wesley.

Levy, D. A. (1997). *Tools of critical thinking: Metathoughts for psychology.* Boston: Allyn & Bacon.

Magee, B. (1998). *The story of philosophy.* New York: DK Publishing.

McPeak, J. E. (1981). *Critical thinking and education.* New York: St. Martin's Press.

Meltzoff, J. (1998). *Critical thinking about research: Psychology and related fields.* Washington, DC: American Psychological Association.

Miller, W. R., & Rollnick, S. (1991). *Motivational interviewing: Preparing people to change addictive behavior.* New York: Guilford.

Moldoveanu, M., & Langer, E. (2002). When "stupid" is smarter than we are: Mindlessness and the attribution of stupidity. In R. J. Sternberg (Ed.), *Why smart people can be so stupid* (pp. 212–231). New Haven, CT: Yale University Press.

Mole, P. (2002, November/December). Are skeptics cynical? Popular misunderstandings of skepticism. *Skeptical Inquirer, 26*(6), 44–48.

Mole, P. (2004, January/February). Fallacies and frustrations: Why skeptics dread conversations with true believers. *Skeptical Inquirer, 28*(1), 30–34.

Moore, B. N., & Parker, R. (1995). *Critical thinking* (4th ed.). Mountain View, CA: Mayfield.

Morris, T. (1999). *Philosophy for dummies.* Foster City, CA: IDG Books.

Morse, R. F. (2001, Fall). Humanism: One activist's view. *Free Inquiry, 21,* 22.

Murray, S., Schwartz, J., & Lichter, S. R. (2001). *It ain't necessarily so: How the media make and unmake the scientific picture of reality.* New York: Rowman & Littlefield.

Myers, D. G. (2004). *Intuition: Its powers and perils.* New Haven, CT: Yale University Press.

Nichell, J. (2005, March/April). Intuition: The case of the unknown daughter. *Skeptical Inquirer, 29*(2), 12–13, 33.

Passmore, J. (1967). *On teaching to be critical.* Boston: Routledge & Kegan Paul.

Patterson, E. M., Sobel, M. B., & Sobel, L. C. (1977). *Emerging concepts of alcohol dependence.* New York: Springer.

Paul, R. W. (1993). *Critical thinking: What every person needs to survive in a rapidly changing world.* Santa Rosa, CA: The Center for Critical Thinking.

Peat, F. D. (2003). *From certainty to uncertainty.* Washington, DC: Joseph Henry.

Peele, S. (1988). Can alcoholism and other drug addiction problems be treated away or is the current treatment binge doing more harm than good? *Journal of Psychoactive Drugs, 20,* 375–383.

Pellegrino, J. W. (1995). Technology in support of critical thinking. *Teaching of Psychology, 22,* 11–12.

Perkins, D. N. (2002). The engine of folly. In R. J. Sternberg (Ed.), *Why smart people can be so stupid* (pp. 64–85). New Haven, CT: Yale University Press.

Piattelli-Palmarini, M. (1994). *Inevitable illusions: How mistakes of reason rule our minds.* New York: Wiley.

Pigliucci, M. (2000). *Tales of the rational: Skeptical essays about nature and science.* Atlanta, GA: Freethought Press.

Pigliucci, M. (2003). Creationism vs. scientism. *Free Inquiry, 23*(3), 32–36.

Pinker, S. (1997). *How the mind works.* New York: Norton.

Pinker, S. (2002). *The blank slate: The modern denial of human nature.* New York: Viking.

Prochaska, J. O., Norcross, J. C., & DiClemente, C. C. (1994). *Changing for good.* New York: Morrow.

Ray, W. J. (2000). *Methods toward a science of behavior and experience.* Belmont, CA: Wadsworth/Thomson.

Raymo, C. (1998). *Skeptics and true believers.*New York: Walker.

Reich, R. (1992). *The work of nations.* New York: Vintage.

Rogers, C. (1957). The necessary and sufficient conditions of therapeutic personality change. *Journal of Consulting Psychology, 21,* 95–103.

Roth, I. (1990). Challenging habits of expectations. In J. Mezirow and Associates (Eds.), *Fostering critical reflection in adulthood* (pp. 116–133). San Francisco: Jossey-Bass.

Ruchlis, H. (1990). *Clear thinking: A practical introduction.* Buffalo, NY: Prometheus Books.

Sagan, C. (1996). *The demon-haunted world: Science as a candle in the dark.* New York: Random House.

Scruton, R. (1996). *An intelligent person's guide to philosophy.* New York: Penguin.

Seligman, M. E. P. (1993). *What you can change & what you can't: The complete guide to successful self-improvement.* New York: Knopf.

Sexton, T. L., Whiston, S. C., Bleuer, J. C., & Walz, G. R. (1997). *Integrating outcome research into counseling practice and training.* Alexandria, VA: American Counseling Association.

Shekerjian, D. (1990). *Uncommon genius: How great ideas are born.* New York: Penguin.

Shermer, M. (1997). *Why people believe weird things*. New York: Freeman.

Shermer, M. (2001). *The borderlands of science: Where science meets nonsense*. New York: Oxford University Press.

Singer, M. T., & Lalich, J. (1996). *"Crazy" therapies: What are they? Do they work?* San Francisco: Jossey-Bass.

Snyder, M., & Thomsen, C. J. (1988). Interactions between therapists and clients: Hypothesis testing and behavioral confirmation. In D. C. Turk & P. Salovey (Eds.), *Reasoning, inference, & judgment in clinical psychology* (pp. 124–152). New York: Free Press.

Sobell, M. B., & Sobell, L. C. (1993). *Problem drinkers: Guided self-change treatment*. New York: Guilford.

Solomon, R. C. (1999). *The joy of philosophy: Thinking thin versus the passionate life*. New York: Oxford University Press.

Stanovich, K. E. (2002). Rationality, intelligence, and levels of analysis in cognitive science. Is dystrationalia possible? In R. J. Sternberg (Ed.), *Why smart people can be so stupid* (pp. 124–158). New Haven, CT: Yale University Press.

Stevenson, L., & Haberman, D. L. (1998). *Ten theories of human nature*. New York: Oxford University Press.

Stewart, D., & Blocker, H. G. (1982). *Fundamentals of philosophy*. New York: Macmillan.

Sutherland, S. (1994). *Irrationality: Why we don't think straight*. New Brunswick, NJ: Rutgers University Press.

Taleff, M. J. (1997). *A handbook to assess and treat resistance in chemical dependency*. Dubuque, IA: Kendall/Hunt.

Taleff, M. J. (2000). Using critical thinking to improve outcomes in substance abuse disorder counseling. *Directions in Mental Health Counseling, 10*(6), 63–72.

Taleff, M. J. (2003). The state of addiction studies education: A cross-sectional survey of national college programs. *Journal of Teaching in the Addictions, 2*(1), 59–66.

Tavris, C., & Wade, C. (1995). *Psychology in perspective*. New York: HarperCollins College Publishers.

Thun, M., Peto, R., Lopez, A. D., Monaco, J. H., Henley, J., Heath, C. W. et al. (1997). Alcohol consumption and mortality among middle-aged and elderly U.S. adults. *The New England Journal of Medicine, 337*, 1705–1714.

Troxell, E. A., & Snyder, W. S. (1976). *Making sense of things: An invitation to philosophy*. New York: St. Martin's Press.

Vivian, F. (1968). *Thinking philosophically: An introduction for students*. London: Chatto & Windus.

Volpicelli, J., & Szalavitz, M. (2000). *Recovery options: The complete guide*. New York: Wiley.

Vos Savant, M. (1993). *The power of logical thinking: Easy lessons in the art of reasoning . . . and hard facts about its abuse in our lives*. New York: St. Martin's Press.

Vyse, S. A. (1997). *Believing in magic: The psychology of superstition*. New York: Oxford University Press.

Wallace, J. (1989). Controlled drinking, treatment effectiveness, and the disease model of addiction: A commentary on the ideological wishes of Stanton Peele. *Journal of Psychoactive Drugs, 22*, 261–280.

Wallace, J. (1996). Theory of 12-step-oriented treatment. In F. Rotgers, D. S. Keller, & J. Morgenstern (Eds.), *Treating substance abuse: Theory and technique* (pp. 13–36). New York: Guilford.

Warburton, N. (2004). *Philosophy: The basics*. London: Routledge.

Wright, R. (1994). *The moral animal: Evolutionary psychology and everyday life*. New York: Vintage.

Wynn, C. M., & Wiggins, A. W. (2001). *Quantum leaps in the wrong direction*. Washington, DC: John Henry Press

Youngson, R. (1998). *Scientific blunders: A brief history of how wrong scientists can sometimes be*. New York: Carroll & Graf.

Index